LEARNING MICRO-PROLOG A PROBLEM-SOLVING APPROACH

Tom Conlon

Computer Education Department
Moray House College of Education
Edinburgh, Scotland

Addison-Wesley Publishing Co, Inc.

Reading, Massachusetts · Menlo Park, California ·
Wokingham, England · Don Mills, Ontario ·
Amsterdam · Sydney · Singapore · Tokyo · Mexico City ·
Bogotá · Santiago · San Juan

Library of Congress Cataloging-in-Publication Data
Conlon, Tom, 1954-
Learning Micro-PROLOG.

Bibliography: p.
Includes index.
1. Micro-PROLOG (Computer program language)
I. Title.
QA76.73.P76C66 1985 005.13'3 85-15051
ISBN 0-201-11241-8

Illustrations by Michael Davidson.
Cover design by Marshall Henrichs.
Typeset by Computerset (MFK) Ltd, Ely, Cambridgeshire.

ABCDEFGHIJ-AL-898765
First printing, September 1985

Preface

This book is based on a course of work which has been written, taught, and extensively re-written over an approximately two-year period. It centers on the programming language PROLOG, and on the use of PROLOG to solve problems. The version used throughout is micro-PROLOG (release 3.1 or later), which is now available for a wide range of hardware such as MS DOS and PC DOS systems including the IBM PC, and most CP/M systems. Micro-PROLOG for various other computers, including the Apple II and the Commodore 64, will be released in the very near future.

My original students were drawn variously from the upper years of secondary education. Naturally, then, I hope that the material between these covers will interest this group. But computers respect neither age nor position, and really there is no reason why anybody should not learn from the book, whether they happen to be following a course of study or not. (The majority of present-day computing professionals, for instance, will find that most of the ideas contained here are new to them.) I have taken for granted no particular knowledge of mathematics or computing, although the book does assume that the reader has access to a PROLOG computer system. This is strongly recommended, although not absolutely necessary.

I believe that the content is worthwhile for two main reasons. The first is that it provides an introduction to a radically different approach to computer programming, one which is powerful, relatively easy to understand and – especially in view of fifth generation computing developments – likely to be of sharply increasing importance. The second reason is that a PROLOG computer system happens to be a marvellous tool for problem-solving, an activity which most human beings (given half a chance) find compelling. Problem-solving is both useful and educational too, but I think the reason why people choose to spend so much time solving problems (with Rubik cubes and adventure games, bridge matches and crosswords, dominoes and chess, crime stories and logic puzzles . . .) is that problem-solving is great fun in its own right. Hopefully, after reading this book you will think so too.

Acknowledgements
Many people have contributed to the ideas which I have tried to present in this book. The influence of both Robert Kowalski and George Polya is especially acknowledged.

Keith Clark of Logic Programming Associates (which has done tremendous work in making PROLOG available on low-cost microcomputers) is to be thanked for his help, as is Paul Fellows of Acornsoft.

Many colleagues and friends have read and commented upon various parts of the manuscript at different stages, and I would like to thank George Connell, Brian Higgins, John McCarney, John McGee, Shiona McDonald, Douglas MacKenzie, Jeremy Nicoll, Margaret Somerville, Robb Sutherland and Tony van der Kuyl.

Peter Barker, my head of department, is to be thanked for his support and unfailing good humour.

Credit is due to the pupils of Jordanhill College School, Glasgow, and Beath High School, Fife, who were the main guinea-pigs in the development of this material, and to the teachers who made it possible.

A large number of teachers and lecturers have been the victims of my attempts to explain PROLOG, and for suffering me without silence I am grateful to them all.

Jean Casey is to be thanked again.

None of the people mentioned above are to blame for any weaknesses or mistakes, whether real or imaginary, which are discovered in this book. These, alas, must be down to me.

Edinburgh
September 1984

Tom Conlon

Contents

1 The problem-solving machine

The history of the modern electronic computer spans less than half a century, but it is a history of dynamic change. We begin with a brief consideration of the place of PROLOG in that history.

TWO STYLES OF PROGRAMMING

A computer is a machine for solving information problems. It is a tool which expands the power of the mind, just as older tools — the lever, the steam engine and the aeroplane, for example — expanded the power of the human body.

To use a computer for problem-solving requires that we communicate with it. At root, this communication is through the activity of **programming**.

One way of programming a computer is to tell the machine exactly what to do. That is, we present it with a **sequence of instructions** which we know will lead to a solution to the problem in which we are interested. Such a program might look like this:

```
1  FOR N = 3 TO 100
2  LET I = 2
3  IF N/I = INT(N/I) THEN 6
4  IF I < SQR(N) THEN LET I = I+1 : GO TO 3
5  PRINT N
6  NEXT N
```

The computer obeys the instructions more or less blindly, like a slave which has been given its commands.

This is the **imperative**[(1)] style of programming. It is the style which has been employed with the first four generations of computers, from the pioneering vacuum-valve machines of the 1940s through to computers which were based in turn on transistors, on the first silicon chips and on the microprocessors of today. A variety of imperative programming languages have been developed, for example BASIC, LOGO, COMAL and Pascal: these languages reflect different ideas about the best ways in which to write the instructions.

The imperative style has been established for so long that many people (especially people who have programmed computers) find it hard to imagine any alternative to it. But an alternative becomes obvious when you ask yourself a simple question. Suppose you have a problem, and you are lucky enough to have access to a really powerful problem-solving machine. How would you actually **like** to be able to communicate with the machine? Most people agree that they would wish to be able to **describe** their problem to the machine in general terms, probably by talking to it in English. The computer should then supply the answer. That, after all, is how we communicate with human problem-solvers such as, say, doctors, lawyers, architects or whomever.

For the moment, let us leave aside the desirability of talking to a computer in English, and concentrate on the idea of communicating any kind of a **description of the problem**. Is the idea feasible? Could a computer solve a problem just on the basis of a description? In theory, yes: providing the description contains all the information which is needed to solve the problem, then a smart enough computer should be able to use it to work out the answer. With such a computer, we would not need to provide instructions telling it **how** to use the information: it would be enough to declare all the relevant aspects of the problem to be solved, and let the machine take over from there.

That is the essence of the **declarative** style of programming.

THE DECLARATIVE APPROACH

What will a program written in the declarative style be like? It should not be too different from the kind of descriptions which are supplied to human problem-solvers. For instance, in communicating a problem to a doctor, a patient will give descriptions like:

The pain is on the right side of my chest.

and:

My head spins if I climb the stairs quickly.

These are statements communicating a **fact** and and a **rule** respectively. A declarative program written for a computer is precisely like this: it is a description which takes the form of **a set of facts and rules**. Let us look at an example of one of these programs. The following is part of a declarative computer program designed to solve medical problems:

```
1 Asthma sufferers should avoid smoky atmospheres.
2 The atmosphere in Ed's Bar and Grille is smoky.
3 Henry is an asthma sufferer.
```

If the problem is:

```
What should Henry avoid?
```

then a computer using this program should be able to answer `Ed's Bar and Grille`. It's quite reasonable to expect the computer to be able to find this answer, since it can be arrived at **by applying logical deduction to the description**. And logical deduction is something which a smart computer should be good at.

Notice however that we should not expect more than is reasonable. The patient in the doctor's surgery can dither, and get confused over the symptoms, and generally mess up the description of the problem; the doctor can usually be relied on to make sense of it all. It would be foolish to put such obstacles in the way of a computer. The declarative approach is more likely to be successful if programs are very precise, ideally written in some language which is tailored for exact logical description. Notice, too, that in solving a problem the doctor adds a large quantity of additional knowledge to the patient's description; logical deduction is applied to the combination of the two. A declarative program for a computer on the other hand will be required to supply **every scrap** of information needed to solve the problem. We can expect that the problem-solving machine is capable of logical deduction, but we mustn't assume that it has access to any more knowledge than that which is contained within its program.

Yet the attractiveness of the declarative approach is clear from a comparison of the two programs shown above. Declarative programs should always be easier to understand. Since they are simply descriptions of problems, and not recipes for solving them, they should be easier to write. The meaning of a declarative program is self-evident, whereas, to understand the meaning of an imperative program, you are forced to think in terms of the behavior which the program will produce on a machine. And the connection between the machine's behavior and the problem which is being solved can be very obscure.

The end result of the declarative approach, of course, should be computers which are more effective problem-solving machines at the service of humankind.

PROLOG AND THE FIFTH GENERATION

Why have the first four generations of computers been programmed imperatively? The short answer is that computers have mainly been too small, too slow and above all too stupid to support the declarative style. But the fifth generation, which is being developed now, promises to overcome these limitations. Exactly what fifth generation computers will be like, nobody yet knows: but it is a very sure bet that, while imperative programming will not disappear, the declarative approach will become increasingly important.

The programming language which is at the center of some of the most important fifth generation developments is called PROLOG. PROLOG — the name stands for 'PROgramming in LOGic' — is the most successful declarative language which has been developed to date. Already it has been used to build expert systems, to analyze natural languages, to prove theorems in mathematics, to construct translators for computers, and to solve problems in a host of other areas. It must be said that PROLOG, as it exists today, falls short of the declarative ideal which has been described above. Its limitations principally mean that programmers cannot altogether ignore the ways in which their descriptions will be used by the computer. In spite of this, a PROLOG computer system is still an enormously powerful problem-solving tool. This we shall discover for ourselves in what follows.

We end this introduction with some PROLOG terms which we shall require immediately. A set of facts and rules which makes up a problem description in PROLOG is called a **program** or **database** (the two words are used interchangeably). Each fact and rule is known as a **sentence**; sentences must be written in a special precise form known as **sentence form**. A question to the computer is called a **query**. A query is really a request that the computer should solve a problem. This it will try to do by applying logical deduction to the sentences in the database.

SUMMARY

(1) Computers are tools for solving problems. The imperative style of programming is concerned with communicating with computers by giving them instructions. The declarative style is concerned with giving descriptions.

(2) A declarative program consists of a set of facts and rules, written in a precise form, which contains the information necessary to solve the problem. The computer solves problems by applying logical deduction to the facts and rules.

(3) PROLOG is the first successful language for declarative programming. It is the core language of important fifth generation computing developments.

NOTES

(1) Literally, 'imperative' means 'commanding'.

2 Writing and using descriptions

The aim of this chapter is to provide an informal introduction to the PROLOG way of writing descriptions. We practice writing facts and rules in sentence form, we find out how to enter a database into the computer, and we make up queries to solve some simple problems.

FACTS AND RULES

Let us pretend that we have arrived at a party. The music is loud, the lights are low and we are among friends. The scene cries out for description — so we shall wander round, gathering facts and rules as we come across them, and writing them down first in English and then in PROLOG.

We quickly notice that Bill is sitting next to Jean, gazing at her admiringly. Clearly Bill likes Jean. That gives us our first fact. In the form of a PROLOG sentence, we write it as:

```
likes(Bill Jean)
```
(1)

The PROLOG and the English versions of the sentence are not all that much different.

Sam, the acting barman, has started to tell us a long gossip story. The details are too complicated to relate, but it can be summed up by writing down two more facts about people who like other people. In PROLOG, the facts are:

```
likes(Diane Colin)                                    (2)
likes(Janet Ian)                                      (3)
```

PROLOG facts have a special structure. They comprise a term by itself called the **predicate** followed by a bracketed list of terms called the **arguments**. Predicates roughly correspond to verbs in English sentences, and arguments correspond to nouns. So far, our facts have all had `likes` as the predicate and the arguments have been the names of individuals. Note that the order of the arguments matters: saying that Diane likes Colin is not the same thing as saying that Colin likes Diane, neither in English nor in PROLOG.

Speaking of arguments, loud voices are coming from one corner of the room. A disagreement has begun over the kind of music which is to be played. Diane is an avid rock fan, while Jean enjoys reggae and Ian favors heavy metal bands. You decide to set down the facts in PROLOG:

```
enjoys(Diane rock)                                    (4)
enjoys(Jean reggae)                                   (5)
enjoys(Ian heavy-metal)                               (6)
```

The predicate here is `enjoys`. The first argument is the name of an individual; the second is the type of music which is enjoyed. Sometimes we use the word **relation** instead of predicate, and say that the above are 'facts for the `enjoys` relation'. Notice the hyphen in `heavy-metal`, making it one term instead of two. Spaces and brackets are used to tell PROLOG where one term ends and another one begins. Putting a hyphen in `heavy-metal` makes it a single term, like `rock` and `reggae`.

Suddenly your eyes start to water and you are coughing. The air has grown thick with tobacco smoke, and you look round for the culprits. Just as you expected: Diane and Ian — the two notorious puffers — are smoking away. The facts are simply described in PROLOG:

```
smokes(Diane)                                                (7)
smokes(Ian)                                                  (8)
```

This time the predicate is `smokes` and the single argument is the name of the smoker.

But smoking is not Diane's only vice. At this very moment, she is being given a large gin and tonic by Sam. It looks as though Sam may have a busy night: he has just given a cola to Colin, and now he is about to fill a glass of white wine for Jean. You note down the facts in PROLOG:

```
gives(Sam Diane gin-and-tonic)                               (9)
gives(Sam Colin cola)                                        (10)
gives(Sam Jean white-wine)                                   (11)
```

Notice again the use of hyphens to ensure that each fact has the same pattern as the other facts for the `gives` relation. It is important to be consistent about the number of arguments and the position of each argument, as will become clear later.

By now the structure of a predicate followed by a list of arguments will be quite familiar. This structure is so fundamental in PROLOG that it is called **atomic**. Anything which has the structure is an **atom**. An atom describes a **relationship** between individuals or objects: a fact is a sentence which asserts that a relationship is true.(1)

Meanwhile, Janet has told you that whenever she smokes, she becomes ill. For her, it is an absolute rule. That gives you a chance to write down your first ever PROLOG rule. A rule has two parts known as the **consequence** part and the **condition** part. It is important to identify each part. In our rule, the consequence that `Janet is ill` holds true on fulfillment of the condition that `Janet smokes`. Turning the consequence and the condition into atoms, we can write `ill(Janet)` and `smokes(Janet)` respectively. Then a PROLOG version of the rule is the sentence:

```
ill(Janet) if smokes(Janet)                                  (12)
```

Every PROLOG rule takes the form of an atom which describes the consequence part of the rule, followed by the word '`if`', followed by the atoms which make up the condition part (joined by the word '`and`' or '`&`' if there is more than one). Sometimes we call the consequence part the **head** and the condition part the **tail** of the rule. As you can see, the correct form (or **syntax**) of a PROLOG rule is very simple, but for the computer to understand the rule the syntax must be followed exactly.

We get our second rule from Jean. She has not yet met Ian, but if he turns out to be a heavy metal fan then she intends to partner him in a dance. You note the consequence part of the rule: it is that `Jean partners Ian`. You note the one condition: that `Ian enjoys heavy metal`. To obtain a PROLOG translation of the rule, we turn these two into atoms and connect them with an '`if`'. So we write:

```
partners(Jean Ian) if enjoys(Ian heavy-metal)                    (13)
```

Jean seems to have started something here. Janet says that she too will partner Ian if he is a heavy metal fan, but she adds the extra condition that Ian must like Bill. You note the consequence: it is that `Janet partners Ian`. You note the two conditions: that `Ian enjoys heavy metal` is one; and that `Ian likes Bill` is the other. Re-writing each of these in atomic form leads to a PROLOG version of the rule:

```
partners(Janet Ian) if                                           (14)
                    enjoys(Ian heavy-metal) &
                    likes(Ian Bill)
```

Setting it down over several lines like this makes the rule a little easier to read. Note that where a rule has more than one condition, as here, **all** the conditions must be true in order to prove that the consequence is true. So Janet might not partner Ian if he is a heavy metal fan but does not like Bill, for instance.

Diane isn't one to be left out of this game. She proclaims that she will partner Sam in a dance if Sam gives her a gin and tonic, on condition also that he does not smoke. You identify the consequence and the two conditions, and you set down Diane's rule as a PROLOG sentence:

```
partners(Diane Sam) if                                           (15)
                    gives(Sam Diane gin-and-tonic) &
                    not smokes(Sam)
```

A set of two or more conditions joined with '`&`' or '`and`' is sometimes called a **conjunction**. The second condition in the conjunction above is an example of a **negation**. A negation is formed by putting the word '`not`' in front of an atom. Negations can appear anywhere in the tail of a rule; but it is one of the restrictions of the PROLOG language that

```
likes(Bill Jean)                                          (1)
likes(Diane Colin)                                        (2)
likes(Janet Ian)                                          (3)

enjoys(Diane rock)                                        (4)
enjoys(Jean reggae)                                       (5)
enjoys(Ian heavy-metal)                                   (6)

smokes(Diane)                                             (7)
smokes(Ian)                                               (8)

gives(Sam Diane gin-and-tonic)                            (9)
gives(Sam Colin cola)                                     (10)
gives(Sam Jean white-wine)                                (11)

ill(Janet) if smokes(Janet)                               (12)

partners(Jean Ian) if enjoys(Ian heavy-metal)             (13)
partners(Janet Ian) if                                    (14)
                  enjoys(Ian heavy-metal) &
                  likes(Ian Bill)
partners(Diane Sam) if                                    (15)
                  gives(Sam Diane gin-and-tonic) &
                  not smokes(Sam)
```

Fig. 2.1 PARTY.

the head of a rule must **not** be a negation. That is, the consequence of a PROLOG rule must always be an atom.

At this juncture we shall leave the party. The cool night air and the quiet comes as a welcome change after all that smoke and noise. In any case, we now have quite an interesting description of the evening in the form of a database which we shall name PARTY. It contains fifteen sentences — eleven facts and four rules — which for convenience are gathered together in Figure 2.1. For now, it's time to find out how we can transfer PARTY from our notepad on to a computer so that PROLOG can use it to solve some problems.[2]

SWITCHING ON

Let us suppose that you are comfortably seated in front of a computer, and that micro-PROLOG is all set up and ready to go (the manual supplied with the PROLOG package will tell you how to do this for your particular computer). Set out below are all the essential points which you need to know in order to enter the PARTY database into your machine.

(a) Adding sentences

The add command (which must be typed in lower case) lets you add a sentence to the database. The sentence must be enclosed in brackets. For example,

```
add(likes(Bill Jean))
```

enters the first PARTY fact into the computer.

Make it a habit to glance at the screen just before you press **RETURN**. Before **RETURN**, you can use your computer's **DELETE** key to fix any errors. Once you have pressed **RETURN** it is harder to make changes.

The add command by itself will put the sentence into the database at the end of any existing sentences for that same relation. Inserting a digit after add lets you put it anywhere else among them. For example,

```
add 2(likes(Diane Colin))
```

will make this fact the second among the sentences for the likes relation.

(b) The prompt

During much of your time at the computer, the screen will display

```
&.
```

This is called the **prompt**. It tells you that PROLOG is waiting for you to type something. (When PROLOG is busy on a problem, no prompt will be visible.) Let us suppose you type a legal command and press RETURN. For an instant, the screen will look like this:

```
&.add(likes(Bill Jean))
```

but then the prompt will re-appear and the screen will show

```
&.add(likes(Bill Jean))
&.
```

Had there been something wrong with the command then an error message would appear telling you so. In the above the re-appearance of the prompt shows that the command has been successfully carried out.

In fact, you aren't bound to wait until the whole command has been typed before pressing RETURN. You could split the command over several lines, pressing RETURN after each line. Providing it's done correctly, the effect will be the same, and PROLOG will try to remind you of where you are after each line by changing the prompt. The new prompt will be a digit telling you how many right brackets are needed to balance the number of left brackets typed so far. For example, you could see

```
&.add(likes(        RETURN
2.Bill Jean))       RETURN
&.
```

The prompt changed to '`2.`' to indicate the need for two right brackets to follow. Prompts of '`1.`' and '`.`' indicate that PROLOG expects input which includes one and zero right brackets respectively.

(c) Listing sentences

The `list` command enables you to check the contents of the current database. Enter `list all` to see everything, or `list gives` (say) to see only the sentences for the `gives` relation.

When you list the sentences of the PARTY database, some of them may appear differently from the way they were entered. This is because some versions of PROLOG internally alter the form of sentences. We'll find out more about this later in the chapter: don't worry about it for now.

(d) Deleting sentences

Sometimes sentences have to be deleted, either because they're wrong or because we no longer need them. This is what the `delete` command is for. Enter

```
delete enjoys 2
```

to delete the second `enjoys` sentence, or

```
delete ill 1
```

to delete the first `ill` sentence (you need the `1` even if it is the **only** `ill` sentence).

(e) Killing sentences

`kill` is more drastic than `delete`. It wipes out **every** sentence for a particular relation. For example,

```
kill partners
```

will remove all the sentences for `partners`. That is, any `partners` facts and all rules in which the consequence part is a `partners` atom will be deleted.

A particularly lethal version of `kill` is `kill all` which wipes out the entire database, letting you start again with a completely fresh slate.

(f) Editing sentences

It often happens that some kind of change needs to be made to one of the database sentences. Instead of deleting the sentence and re-entering it from scratch, you can use `edit`. The command

```
edit smokes 2
```

will display the second `smokes` sentence ready for you to modify using your computer's editing keys. To edit the first `ill` sentence, enter

```
edit ill 1
```

(again, you must type the 1). The details of how to edit depend on your computer: look up the `edit` command in your PROLOG reference manual and practice with it on your machine.

(g) Saving and loading a database

Typing is hard work. Once you have entered the fifteen PARTY sentences into your machine, you can save them permanently on to disk with the command

```
save PARTY
```

Then should there be a loss of power, or should you want to use the same database again in a month's time, you have a copy safely stored away. The command

```
load PARTY
```

re-enters the sentences back into the computer's memory. For more information about loading and saving databases, look at the PROLOG reference manual for your computer.

Choose a name other than PARTY if you like. The main restriction is that the name chosen must differ from the names of each of your database relations.

(h) Interrupting PROLOG

Now and again you will want to interrupt PROLOG and restore the familiar '&.' prompt. This could be because the prompt has changed to '.' and you have lost track of what input is expected of you, for instance. On CP/M and MS and PC DOS systems, pressing CTRL with C does this job. Pressing CTRL with C will restore the prompt and the sentences in your database will not be affected.

FORMING `is`-QUERIES

Now that the PARTY database has been entered into your computer, PROLOG can be asked to use the description to solve some problems. Our first problem is not very great (unless you happen to be Janet or Ian): it is to find out whether Janet likes Ian. If you enter

```
is(likes(Janet Ian))
```

then the problem will be immediately solved by PROLOG's response:

```
YES
```

A question in PROLOG is called a **query** and the query we have just formed is an example of an `is`-query. The idea of an `is`-query is to find out whether a relationship, represented by an atom, is true or false. The answer here was `YES` because this atom is identical to one of the facts in the database. The atom is often called the **goal** of the query: it is what PROLOG has to try to deduce. When the answer is `YES`, as here, then we say that the goal **succeeded** or that the goal was **satisfied**.

To solve the problem of whether Bill smokes, try

```
is(smokes(Bill))
```

and `NO` will come back in reply. The goal this time was `smokes(Bill)` and the answer was `NO` because the goal could not be deduced from the database.

Now let us solve the problem we have all been thinking about. Does Jean partner Ian in a dance or does she not? Enter

```
is(partners(Jean Ian))
```

and we get

```
YES
```

So now we know! Solving this problem involved a little more work for PROLOG than `likes(Janet Ian)`, which matched the fact at sentence 3 thereby giving an immediate answer. `partners(Jean Ian)` matched the head of the rule at sentence 13, so PROLOG had to check whether the condition of the rule, namely `enjoys(Ian heavy-metal)`, could be proved. PROLOG then found the match between the condition and the fact at sentence 6. Thus the goal of the query succeeded.

Naturally, we also want to solve the problem of whether Diane partners Sam. The query to try this time is

```
is(partners(Diane Sam))
```

To answer the question, PROLOG matches the query goal with the head of the rule at sentence 15, the tail of which is

```
gives(Sam Diane gin-and-tonic) & not smokes(Sam)
```

The first of these conditions is proved by sentence 9. PROLOG then tries to find a match for `smokes(Sam)` and, on failing, it decides that `not smokes(Sam)` must be true. So both conditions are found true, and PROLOG answers `YES` to the query. PROLOG's built-in deduction is so fast that the response seems almost instantaneous.

This last example illustrates something important about the way PROLOG handles negations. In logical argument of the ordinary kind, it would be wrong to conclude that Sam **does not** smoke simply because we can't prove that he **does** smoke. (There are people who only smoke when nobody else is looking.) Yet this is PROLOG's logic. It considers that **something is false if it cannot be proved**. This assumption is correct as long as the database contains everything that needs to be known about the problem to be solved. For example, if it is certain that the name of every smoker is recorded in a corresponding `smokes` fact, then the absence of `smokes(Sam)` will indeed prove that Sam is a non-smoker. Usually, PROLOG's simplified approach to negation is perfectly adequate, but we should bear in mind that it is a simplification.

Exercise

Express these problems as `is`-queries to the PARTY database. Try to anticipate the answers, and check your understanding by typing them into a PROLOG computer which has PARTY as its current database.

(a) Is it true that Diane likes Colin?

(b) Does Jean enjoy rock?
(c) Is Ian a smoker?
(d) Does Janet smoke?
(e) Does Sam give Colin a cola?
(f) Is Tom ill?
(g) Is Janet ill?
(h) Does Janet partner Ian in a dance?
(i) Does Sam partner Diane?
(j) Is Jean given white wine to drink by Sam?

FORMING WHICH-QUERIES

Many problems cannot be solved just by `YES` or `NO`. For example, the solution to a problem might be the name of an individual. These problems require us to use the `which` form of query. As an example, if we wanted to know which individuals smoke, we could enter

```
which(x : smokes(x))
```

This query is asking: 'Which term could replace `x` in the goal `smokes(x)` in order to make the goal succeed?'. PROLOG will reply:

```
Diane
Ian
No (more) answers
```

The `x` in the query is an example of a **variable**. A variable stands for an unknown term. In the query above, the terms `Diane` and `Ian` are possible replacements for `x`, since when they replace the variable in the goal the result is an atom which is identical to a fact in the database. This is why these two names are displayed on the screen. To show that no **other** replacements for `x` could be found, PROLOG ends with the '`No (more) answers`' message.(3)

To find out whom Bill likes, we could ask

```
which(x : likes(Bill x))
```

We get back:

```
Jean
No (more) answers
```

since `Jean` is the only replacement for `x` which makes `likes(Bill x)` true.

We used a variable named `x` in both the queries above. Actually, it could have been any one of these:

```
X Y Z x y z X1 Y1 Z1 x1 y1 z1 X2 Y2 Z2 x2 y2 z2 X3 Y3 ...
```

although the answers to the queries would have been the same whichever variable had been selected. A variable in a list of arguments simply holds a place which can be filled by any suitable term.

But the **position** occupied by a variable within a query goal **does** matter. The query

```
which(x : likes(x Bill))
```

is different from the last query. It asks: 'Who likes Bill?'. The answer this time will be

```
No (more) answers
```

which means that **no** replacements for `x` could be found which made the goal succeed. As another example, to see who gets a cola from Sam we have to ask

```
which(x : gives(Sam x cola))
```

It would **not** be correct to ask

```
which(x : gives(Sam cola x))
```

since here the arguments of the goal atom are positioned differently from those of the `gives` facts in the database. You can see now why it is important to be consistent about the pattern of arguments for each predicate at the time sentences are written.

Sometimes it is necessary to use more than one variable in a query goal. To find out who is given some kind of drink by Sam, we could query

```
which(x : gives(Sam x y))
```

We don't care **which** drink is given, and so we make the third argument a variable (we used `y`, but any variable other than `x` would do equally well) which will match any kind of drink. Because only `x` appears to the left of the colon, only the replacements for that variable will be printed out as answers. PROLOG will reply:

```
Diane
Colin
Jean
No (more) answers
```

Had we **also** wanted to know the corresponding replacements for `y`, we would have queried

```
which(x y :  gives(Sam x y))
```

This would have produced

```
Diane gin-and-tonic
Colin cola
Jean white-wine
No (more) answers
```

The terms which appear between the bracket and the colon in a `which`-query are together known as the **answer pattern**. To answer the query PROLOG tries to find replacements for the variables in the goal which make the goal succeed. Each time this happens, an answer is printed on the screen in the form of the replacements for those variables which appear in the answer pattern. For example, the query goal `gives(Sam x y)` above succeeded when `x` was replaced by `Diane` and `y` by `gin-and-tonic`, and since `x` and `y` appear in the answer pattern PROLOG displays these replacements on the screen.

An answer pattern may include English words among the variables. In this case PROLOG just inserts the same words, in the same order, when it displays replacements. For example, the query

```
which(x has y to drink :  gives(Sam x y))
```

produces the answers

```
Diane has gin-and-tonic to drink
Colin has cola to drink
Jean has white-wine to drink
No (more) answers
```

Answers like these are a little more self-explanatory.

A `which`-query (and an `is`-query too) may contain a conjunction of goals. For example,

```
which(x : enjoys(x rock) & smokes(x))
```

This query asks: 'Who enjoys rock and also smokes?'. The same variable x appears in both goals, and so PROLOG must find a replacement for it which satisfies them both. In this case we get

```
Diane
No (more) answers
```

The query

```
which(x : likes(y x) & gives(Sam x z))
```

asks: 'Who is liked by someone and is also given something to drink by Sam?'. Here, x represents the individual whose identity we want to discover. We don't care who the 'someone' is or what the 'something' might be, so we let a couple of variables (any couple, as long as they differ from each other and they differ from x) act as place-fillers. PROLOG's answer will be

```
Jean
Colin
No (more) answers
```

Occasionally, a slightly modified version of the `which`-query called `one` is useful. If you try the queries above using `one` in place of `which` you will get the same answers, but they appear one at a time and you have the option of abandoning the query after the display of each answer.

Exercise

Translate these problems into `which`-queries to the PARTY database. Try to anticipate the answers, and then check your understanding by trying them out on a computer.

(a) Who likes Ian?
(b) Whom does Janet like?

(c) What type of music is enjoyed by Jean?
(d) What is Colin given to drink by Sam?
(e) Who is ill?
(f) Whom does Jean partner?
(g) What kinds of music are enjoyed?
(h) Who likes whom?
(i) Who is liked by someone and also smokes?
(j) Who smokes and likes someone?
(k) Who partners whom?
(l) Who enjoys some kind of music and does not smoke?

VARIABLES IN RULES

We have seen how useful variables are in queries. A variable represents an unspecified term: it is the PROLOG equivalent of a word like 'someone', 'anything' or 'something' in English. Words like these often appear in English rules, such as

Someone is unhealthy if they smoke.

To write such a rule in PROLOG, we need to use a variable. Writing x in place of the 'someone' referred to in the rule, we can write the consequence part of the above in PROLOG as

```
unhealthy(x)
```

and the condition as

```
smokes(x)
```

So a PROLOG version of the rule could be

```
unhealthy(x) if smokes(x)                    (16)
```

Note that this sentence holds good **for every possible replacement** for x. For example, it follows that all these rules are true:

```
unhealthy(Ian) if smokes(Ian)
unhealthy(Janet) if smokes(Janet)
unhealthy(Colin) if smokes(Colin)
```

and even

```
unhealthy(reggae) if smokes(reggae)
```

and so on. Each one of these is called an **instance** of the general rule. Indeed, we could replace the general rule completely by writing all the instances of it instead — but since we would need one instance for every possible term, this would involve a lot of hard work. We prefer instead to write just one general rule which uses a variable to represent the terms.

We have numbered the sentence above because we intend to add it with the `add` command to the PARTY database. We can then ask: 'Who is unhealthy?' with the query

```
which(x : unhealthy(x))
```

PROLOG will solve this problem in no time:

```
Diane
Ian
No (more) answers
```

To find these replacements for `x`, PROLOG used the new sentence. The sentence tells it: 'To find replacements for `x` in `unhealthy(x)`, find replacements for `x` in `smokes(x)`'. Now the facts at sentences 7 and 8 show that `Diane` and `Ian` are such replacements, and so the two notorious puffers are identified as answers.

If, after entering the rule above, you now inspect it again with the `list` command, you may notice that something odd has happened. PROLOG has re-named the variable in the sentence from `x` to `X`. In fact PROLOG ignores your original choice of variables in a sentence, and inserts substitutes for them according to a scheme of its own. The first variable appearing in the sentence is always re-named to `X`, the second to `Y`, then `Z`, `x`, `y`, `z` and so on. This is a little disturbing at first: but of course it makes no difference to the meaning of your sentence, since it is the **positions** in which variables appear in a sentence which counts and not the names given to the variables. Notice however that when you change a sentence using the `edit` command, it is PROLOG's version of the sentence which you must amend.

Another rule which we shall add is

Somebody is popular if anyone likes them.

We need two different variables for this rule, since the 'somebody' is not generally the same as the 'anyone'. Let us use x and y. Then the consequence of the rule can be written as popular(x) and the condition as likes(y x). So the PROLOG version is

```
popular(x) if likes(y x)                                    (17)
```

If we now ask

```
which(x :  popular(x))
```

then the new rule will show PROLOG how to answer the query. The rule says: 'To find replacements for x in popular(x), find replacements for x in likes(y x)'. Now suitable such replacements are found using the facts at sentences 1, 2 and 3, so the computer responds

```
Jean
Colin
Ian
No (more) answers
```

Notice in passing that a variable named x appeared in both the last two rules. However, they are **different** variables. Variables in different sentences have no connection with one another, even if they have the same name.

The last rule we shall add was suggested by Diane. Her rule is

> Everybody who enjoys some kind of music and smokes should partner Diane in a dance.

Letting x represent 'everybody' and z represent 'some music', we can write the consequence here as partners(x Diane) and the two conditions as enjoys(x z) and smokes(x) respectively. So in PROLOG, Diane's rule could be written as

```
partners(x Diane) if                                        (18)
                    enjoys(x z)  &
                    smokes(x)
```

Now we can solve the obvious problem of which individual is going to dance with Diane:

```
which(x : partners(x Diane))
```

The solutions are

```
Diane
Ian
No (more) answers
```

Perhaps Diane didn't expect to be told that she must dance with herself in order to obey her own rule — but PROLOG's logic is faultless if you think about it!

Exercise

Write PROLOG versions of the following rules, and add them to the PARTY database. (In some cases you will have to invent suitable predicates.) Try out each rule with some suitable queries.

(a) Someone is sensible if they like Colin.
(b) Anyone is glad if Janet likes them.
(c) Everybody who enjoys heavy metal is hard of hearing.
(d) Someone is lively if they enjoy reggae.
(e) A drink is expensive if it is given to someone by Sam.
(f) Ian is jealous of anyone whom Diane likes.
(g) Someone who smokes and enjoys heavy metal is odd.
(h) Sam detests a person who is popular and does not smoke.
(i) Everyone remembers someone who partners them in a dance.
(j) A person who smokes and is not liked by anyone is miserable.

MORE ABOUT ATOMS AND TERMS

The atomic structure of a predicate followed by a list of arguments is very important. We have seen that atoms occur as facts, such as

```
gives(Sam Colin cola)
```

and also as the consequence and the conditions of a rule, as in

```
partners(x Diane) if
                    enjoys(x z)  &
                    smokes(x)
```

Atoms also occur as the goals of queries, for example

```
which(x : popular(x))
```

In this section we look at atoms more closely. We first examine the kinds of term from which they are constructed, and then we look at alternative ways of writing atoms down.

Four kinds of term

Atoms are constructed from terms. There are four different types of term in PROLOG: **words, numbers, variables** and **lists**. The predicate of an atom is always a word; the arguments can be terms of any type. Let us examine each of these four types of term.

(a) WORDS are generally English words, perhaps with hyphens. Each of these counts as one word:

```
likes, ill, Janet, heavy-metal, gin-and-tonic
```

A word must begin with a letter and may not include spaces (spaces tell PROLOG where one term ends and the next term begins, remember). Upper-case letters and lower-case letters are recognised as different: `Sam` and `sam` are different words.

(b) NUMBERS are what you would expect. These are all numbers:

12, 31267, 4.6, 0, –45.66, 6.7E6

(The last of these is a number in 'scientific notation'. It is equivalent to 6.7×10^6, or 6700000).

(c) VARIABLES are any of these:

```
X Y Z x y z X1 Y1 Z1 x1 y1 z1 ...
```

Variables represent unspecified terms.

(d) LISTS are sequences of terms in brackets. Each of these is a list:

```
(Ian Bill Colin), (x 23 West), ()
```

the last being the list of zero terms which is known as the 'empty list'. A list counts as only a single term no matter how long it happens to be. Lists are very important in PROLOG programming and we shall investigate them in depth before long.

Three forms of atom

All the atoms encountered so far have taken this form:

```
partners(Janet Ian)
```

That is, the predicate has come **before** a list of arguments. This syntax is known as the **prefix** form. Actually, PROLOG also recognizes two other forms, known as **infix** (where the predicate is placed **between** two arguments) and **postfix** (where the predicate comes **after** a single argument). The purpose of having these extra atomic forms is really just to provide some variety. Below, we look at the three forms of atom in detail.

(1) PREFIX FORM is the form we have used up until now. The atom is written with the predicate followed by the list of arguments, such as

```
gives(Sam Janet cola)
```

Prefix form is the most general form, in so far as **every** atom can be written this way. Furthermore an atom with more than two arguments can **only** be written like this (which is one reason for learning the prefix form before the others).

(2) INFIX FORM is only for atoms which have **two** arguments, such as the atom

```
enjoys(Jean reggae)
```

In the infix version, the atom is written with the first argument to the left of the predicate and the second argument to the right. The brackets disappear. So

```
Jean enjoys reggae
```

is the infix way of writing it. **There is no difference in meaning** between the two forms. They are equivalent: in any command, query or sentence where `enjoys(Jean reggae)` appears, we can insert `Jean enjoys reggae` with exactly the same effect. So why bother to learn infix? The reason is that this form is often easier and more natural to read and write. From now on, whenever we meet atoms which have two arguments we will generally use the infix form.

(3) POSTFIX FORM is only for atoms which have **one** argument. Instead of writing

```
smokes(Diane)
```

the postfix form puts the predicate after the argument, without brackets. So

```
Diane smokes
```

is the postfix way of writing the atom. Again, note that **there is no difference in meaning** between the two. They are equivalent. But again, we often prefer the postfix form since it is a little more natural.

Having worked hard to learn the prefix form of an atom, perhaps you are now depressed at the thought of having to learn two other forms! In theory, you could if you like stick to prefix form all the time. Unlike infix and postfix, prefix is always available. However, in some versions of PROLOG the `list` and `edit` commands use the infix and postfix forms to display atoms with two arguments and one argument respectively, regardless of how these atoms were entered; this explains why some of the sentences of PARTY may have looked different when you listed them earlier. Suppose for example you add this sentence to a database:

```
speeding(x) if
              drives-at(x y)  &
              faster-than(y 70)
```

When later you list it back, the rule may re-appear as

```
X speeding if
             X drives-at Y  &
             Y faster-than 70
```

where the names of variables and the atomic forms have been internally altered by PROLOG. In spite of the changed appearance, the meaning of the sentence is still exactly the same as before.

Exercise

Identify the predicate and the arguments of each atom in the following sentences, and say what kind of term each argument is. Then re-write each sentence using an alternative form for each atom wherever possible.

(a) `partners(Jean Ian)`

(b) `ill(Janet) if smokes(Janet)`

(c) `Santa delivers presents`

(d) `Mary smiles if Mary rides bicycle`

(e)
```
frightens(werewolf x) if
                  human(x)  &
                  not carries(x cross)
```

(f) `eats(werewolf piglet)`

(g) `y is-sensible if y studies logic`

(h) `x retires if x age 65`

(i)
```
x grandchild-of y if
                x child-of z  &
                z child-of y
```

(j) `x lives-at Ten-Downing-Street if x is-prime-minister`

(k) `lives-on(y Wimbledon-Common) if is-a-womble(y)`

SUMMARY

Figures 2.2–2.4 will help you to remember the summary points of this chapter.

(1) A description in PROLOG takes the form of a database (program) which is made up of a set of facts and rules.

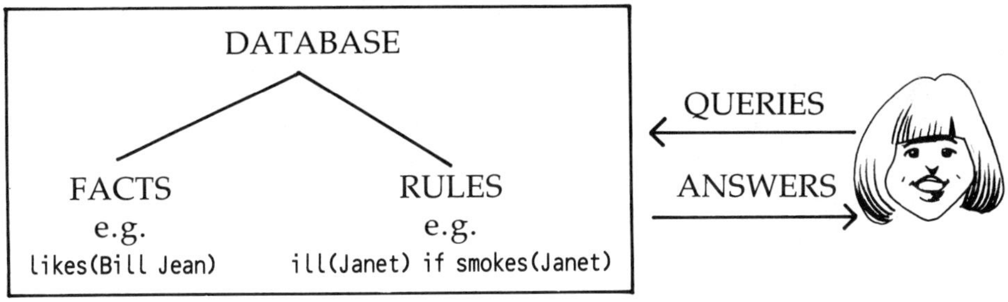

Fig. 2.2

(2) Facts and rules must be written in the precise syntax of sentence form, in which:
- — A fact is a sentence consisting of a single atom.
- — A rule is a sentence consisting of an atom followed by '`if`', followed by any number of atoms or negations connected by '`&`' or '`and`'.

(3) A negation comprises '`not`' followed by an atom.

(4) An atom describes a relationship. It consists of a predicate together with a number of arguments, and is written either in the prefix, infix or postfix form. The predicate must be a word; the arguments may be terms of any type — words, numbers, variables or lists.

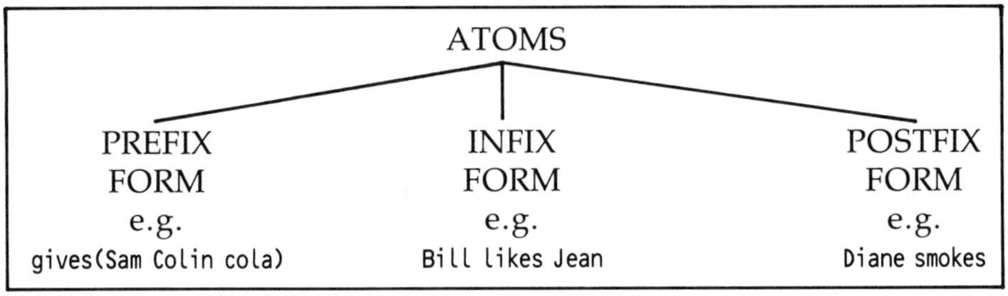

Fig. 2.3

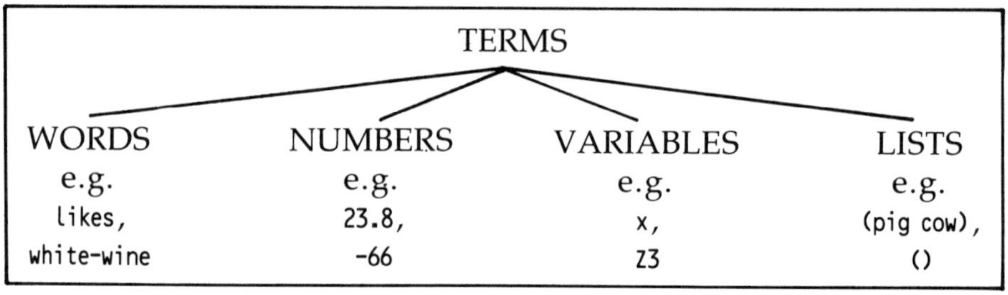

Fig. 2.4

(5) The two main types of query are `is`-queries and `which`-queries. An `is`-query is answered `YES` or `NO`. A `which`-query is answered by replacements for variables in the answer pattern which make the query goal succeed.

NOTES

(1) Strictly speaking, we should call a predicate such as `smokes` which has only one argument a **property**. We ought to say, for instance, that 'Diane has the `smokes` property'. However, to simplify matters we shall refer to all predicates as **relations** no matter how many arguments they have.

(2) 'PROLOG' here refers to 'a PROLOG computer system' and not to the PROLOG language — I hope that the context will always make the meaning clear.

(3) The same message is used whether the number of answers has been none, one or several. The '`(more)`' in the message is intended to make it roughly sensible in all these cases.

3 How PROLOG solves goals

In the last chapter we saw that PROLOG has a built-in deduction capability which enables it to solve problems using a database description. Now we look more closely at that capability. By understanding how PROLOG finds solutions, we will be in a better position to write descriptions which the computer can use successfully.

EVALUATING GOALS WITH FACTS

A key idea which we encountered in the last chapter is the idea of a **goal**.

Everybody knows what is meant when a soccer player talks about a goal: in that game, scoring goals is the main aim. In fact, the word 'goal' in the wider sense literally means an 'aim' or an 'end' to be striven for. A goal in the PROLOG context has the related but slightly special meaning of a **problem to be solved**. An attempt to solve the problem is called a **goal evaluation**. In this section we focus on the way in which PROLOG evaluates goals using only facts: the use of rules will be considered later. To illustrate the points, the SPORT database of facts shown in Figure 3.1 will be used.

```
Helen plays squash                    (1)
Tony plays squash                     (2)
Tony plays soccer                     (3)
Tony plays baseball                   (4)
George plays football                 (5)
Ian plays baseball                    (6)
Alison plays tennis                   (7)
Alison plays squash                   (8)

soccer played-with ball               (9)
squash played-with racket             (10)
squash played-with ball               (11)
football played-with ball             (12)
baseball played-with bat              (13)
baseball played-with ball             (14)
baseball played-with bases            (15)
tennis played-with racket             (16)
tennis played-with ball               (17)
```

Fig. 3.1 SPORT.

Evaluating single atom goals

Physically, a goal is just an atom or a negation. To begin with we shall leave negations aside and consider goals such as

(a) `Helen plays x`
(b) `y played-with ball`
(c) `Ian plays football`
(d) `x1 plays x2`

which are atoms.

The meaning of a goal depends on whether or not it contains variables.

(i) A goal without variables represents the problem: 'Is this relationship true?'. PROLOG evaluates the goal by searching the database from the top, looking for facts which have the same predicate as the goal. If such a fact is found then PROLOG compares corresponding arguments to see if they are identical. The goal is said to **succeed** if a matching fact is found; otherwise it **fails**. An `is`-query containing the goal will report `YES` or `NO` accordingly.

(ii) A goal which contains variables represents the problem: 'For what replacements for the variables is this relationship true?'. PROLOG searches the database from the top as before, looking for facts with the same predicate, but this time in comparing arguments it replaces any arguments which are variables with corresponding terms in an attempt to make the goal and the fact identical. If this is possible then the goal is said to **succeed** with this set of replacements, and we say that the replacements **satisfy** or give a **solution** to the goal. A `which`-query containing the goal will print such solutions on the screen.

As examples, let us evaluate the goals listed above with the SPORT database.

(a) The goal `Helen plays x` has just one solution:

```
x = squash.
```

PROLOG will check all the facts with the `plays` predicate, but only the fact at sentence 1 has a first argument `Helen` which matches the first argument of the goal. The replacement `x = squash` for the second argument then makes the goal and the fact identical.

(b) The goal `y played-with ball` has the solutions

```
y = soccer;
y = squash;
y = football;
y = baseball;
y = tennis.
```

Each replacement for `y` makes the goal identical to one of the facts for the `played-with` relation.

(c) The goal `Ian plays football` fails. PROLOG works down all the `plays` facts in turn, but none of them is identical to the goal and since the goal contains no variables it is not possible to make replacements.

(d) The goal `x1 plays x2` has eight solutions. The first is given by the fact at sentence 1, which has the `plays` predicate and which has arguments which can be made identical to the arguments of the goal by making the set of replacements `x1 = Helen, x2 = squash`. Altogether the solutions are

```
x1 = Helen,  x2 = squash;     x1 = Tony,   x2 = squash;
x1 = Tony,   x2 = soccer;     x1 = Tony,   x2 = baseball;
x1 = George, x2 = football;   x1 = Ian,    x2 = baseball;
x1 = Alison, x2 = tennis;     x1 = Alison, x2 = squash.
```

To check that PROLOG's evaluation of the goals is the same as the ones given here, enter SPORT into your computer and try out the queries

```
which(x :  Helen plays x)
which(y :  y played-with ball)
is(Ian plays football)
which(x1 x2 :  x1 plays x2)
```

Evaluating negations

To evaluate a goal which is a negation, say

```
not George plays squash
```

PROLOG evaluates the goal

```
George plays squash
```

If this goal fails, then the negation is considered to have succeeded; if it succeeds, the negation is considered to have failed. In this case `George plays squash` fails (it cannot be made identical to any of the facts for the `plays` relation) and so the goal `not George plays squash` succeeds. You can check this with the query

```
is(not George plays squash)
```

to which PROLOG will respond YES.

In general, the goal

not <atom>

is intended to represent the problem: 'Is this relationship (i.e. the one associated with <atom>) false?'. The goal will be evaluated by evaluating <atom> as a goal and reversing the outcome: if <atom> succeeds then not <atom> fails, and if <atom> fails then not <atom> succeeds. It follows that the problem which a negation represents is more accurately expressed as: 'Is this relationship one **which cannot be proved from the database**?'.

Let us consider some more examples, again using the SPORT database of facts.

(a) The goal not baseball played-with bat fails, because baseball played-with bat succeeds (it is identical to the fact at sentence 13).

(b) The goal not Alison plays x fails. The reason is that Alison plays x as a goal succeeds (the replacement x = tennis for instance makes it identical to the fact at sentence 7).

(c) The goal not X plays golf succeeds, because X plays golf fails — no replacement for X can make it identical to any plays fact.

You can confirm that PROLOG's evaluations agree with these ones by trying the queries

```
is(not baseball played-with bat)
is(not Alison plays x)
is(not X plays golf)
```

and checking for yourself that the answers are NO, NO and YES respectively.

As we indicated in the last chapter, PROLOG's treatment of negation is a simplification. A good illustration is the YES response to this last query: PROLOG seems to be saying with this answer that

> It is false that
> there exists a person X who plays golf.

Lee Trevino, Arnold Palmer, Tom Watson and a few others might quarrel with this one. Of course, everything becomes clear when we interpret PROLOG's response more accurately. What the YES really means is that

> It cannot be proved from the database that
> there exists a person X who plays golf.

We have to remember that everything really depends on the database containing all the information which will be needed to solve our problems.

The way in which negations are evaluated introduces an important restriction. **A negation cannot be used to generate replacements for variables**. To illustrate this, enter the query

```
which(x :  not Alison plays x)
```

We might wish this query to be answered with the names of games which are not played by Alison (perhaps soccer, baseball and so on) but instead PROLOG just comes back with

```
No (more) answers
```

Why are no replacements found? It is because the query asks

> Find all the replacements for x which
> solve the goal not Alison plays x.

and there are none, because the goal fails (as we saw above). As another example, try the query

```
which(X :  not X plays golf)
```

PROLOG does **not** respond with the names of people who do not play golf. It only reports X followed by No (more) answers.(1) That is, the query goal succeeded (as it did with the `is`-query earlier) but the variable `X` has not been replaced. This is because the **way** the goal succeeds is by showing that `X plays golf` fails. PROLOG cannot answer with replacements for `X`, because it never found any. And if it had found some, then the query goal would not have succeeded!

If all this seems confusing, don't worry. The main thing to remember is that negations are fine for **checking** whether a goal succeeds or fails. But **don't** expect a negation to **generate** answers!

Evaluating conjunctions

A conjunction of goals, such as

```
George plays x  &  x played-with y
```

or

```
x played-with ball  &  not Tony plays x
```

represents the problem: 'For what replacements for variables are all the relationships in the conjunction true?'. By inspecting the database, we can easily evaluate these conjunctions. The first example has only one solution, which is given by the pair of replacements:

```
x = football, y = ball.
```

This set of replacements satisfies both the goals in the conjunction. The second of the above has two solutions:

```
x = football;
x = tennis.
```

To confirm that PROLOG's evaluations agree with these ones, try the queries

```
which(x y :  George plays x  &  x played-with y)
```

and

```
which(x :  x played-with ball  &  not Tony plays x)
```

respectively.

In general, a conjunction of one or more goals

<goal$_1$> & <goal$_2$> & ... & <goal$_k$>

is called a **goal statement**. A goal statement succeeds only if all of the goals within it succeeds: if just one individual goal fails, then so does the whole goal statement. A **solution** to the goal statement is a set of replacements for its variables which makes the goal statement succeed.

In theory, the goals in a goal statement could be evaluated in parallel, or one at a time in any order. It should make no difference to the outcome which method is followed. Unfortunately, our existing computers can only perform one task at a time. They are **sequential** machines, which excludes the possibility of parallel evaluation.(2) Hence, the only question is: In what order does PROLOG evaluate the goals of a conjunction?

We may be able to guess the answer to this question by studying the order in which answers to queries are generated. Try for example the query to the SPORT database:

```
which(x y :  Tony plays x  &  x played-with y)
```

and examine the sequence in which the answers appear:

```
squash  racket
squash  ball
soccer  ball
baseball  bat
baseball  ball
baseball  bases
No (more) answers
```

Figure 3.2 shows the order of evaluation which gave rise to this sequence of answers. The first solution which PROLOG discovers to the first goal `Tony plays x` is `x = squash` using sentence 2. Holding on to this replacement for `x`, the second goal then becomes `squash played-with y`. This is first solved using sentence 10 by the replacement `y = racket`, so making

```
x = squash, y = racket
```

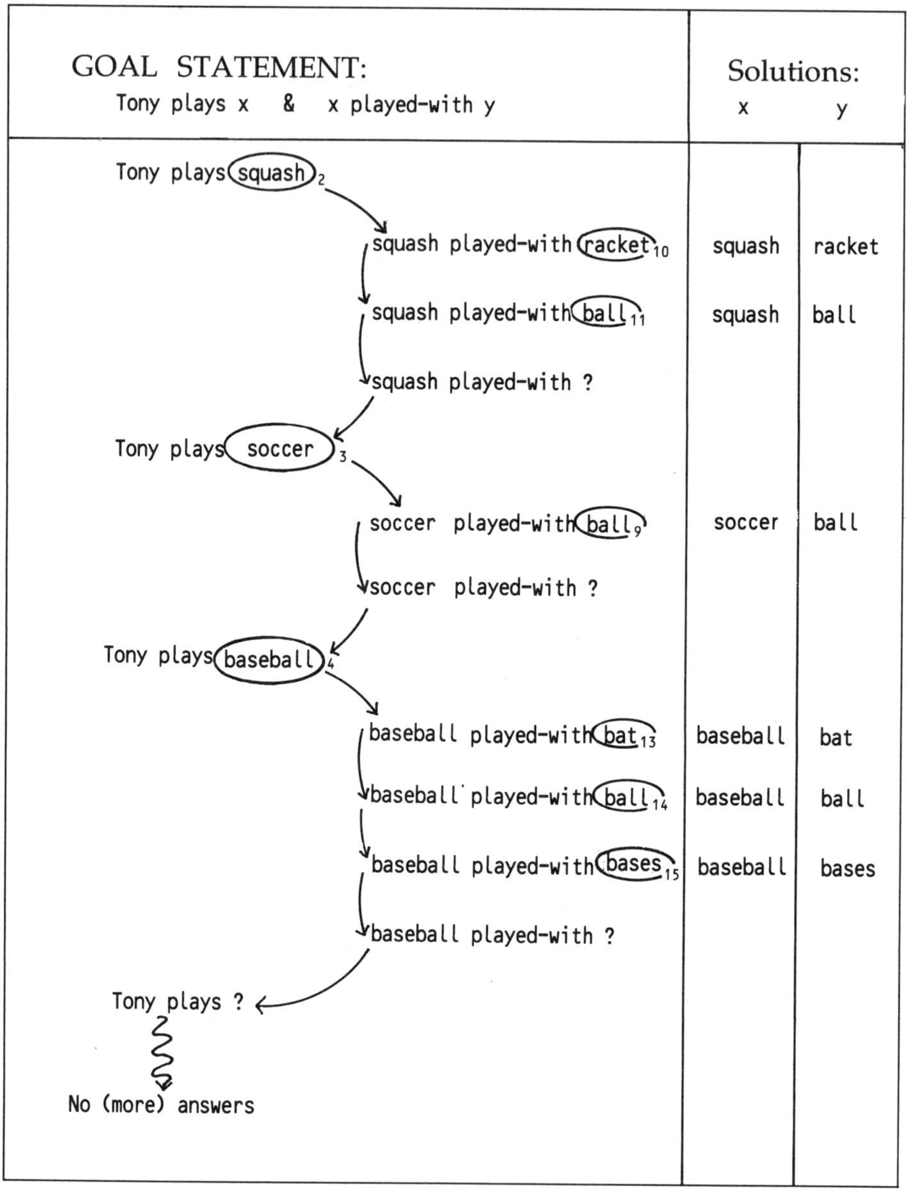

Fig. 3.2

the first solution to the goal statement, and then again by `y = ball` at sentence 11, making

```
x = squash, y = ball
```

the second solution. There are no further solutions to `squash played-with y`, and so PROLOG abandons the replacement `x = squash` and returns to the first goal. An alternative solution to it is sought, below sentence 2 where the goal last succeeded. The solution `x = soccer` is then discovered at sentence 3. Carrying this new replacement forward, the second goal now becomes `soccer played-with y` which is solved by `y = ball` using sentence 9. That makes

```
x = soccer, y = ball
```

the third solution to the goal statement. By following Figure 3.2 in this way through to `No (more) answers` you can re-create the precise manner in which PROLOG found the answers to our query.

A striking feature of Figure 3.2 is the presence of long right and left arrows depicting PROLOG's behaviour as it moves from one goal to another. The right arrows represent **forward-tracking**: when a goal succeeds, PROLOG 'tracks forward' to the next goal carrying with it all the replacements for variables which have so far been made. The left arrows on the other hand depict **back-tracking**: when a goal fails, PROLOG goes back to the previous goal and tries to find an alternative solution to it.

This forward- and back-tracking method of finding solutions to a conjunction of goals is called a **depth-first search.**[3] Although our example involved a goal statement containing two goals which was solved with a database of facts, the same depth-first search strategy is employed for any length of goal statement, and whether goals are solved by facts or by rules makes no difference.

Figure 3.3 gives a detailed account of the depth-first search procedure. An easy way to remind yourself of it is to remember the summary:

forward-track with replacements, back-track for alternatives

Which strategy did you employ, when you evaluated mentally the goal statements at the start of this section? A depth-first search is the most natural choice sometimes, but not always. With a goal statement such as

```
x played-with y  &  Ian plays x
```

it makes more sense to solve the second goal first. Or again, with a

GOAL STATEMENT: <goal$_1$> & <goal$_2$> & ... & <goal$_k$>

(1) Goals are evaluated from left to right.

(2) When a goal succeeds:

(a) If it is not the last goal, forward-track. That is, move to the next goal and try to solve it from the top of the database, taking into account all the replacements which have been made so far.

(b) If it is the last goal, try to solve it again. Each such solution gives a solution to the whole goal statement, in the form of the current set of replacements for variables.

(3) When a goal fails:

(a) If it is not the first goal, back-track. That is, return to the previous goal and abandon the replacements made when it last succeeded. Try to find an alternative solution lower in the database.

(b) If it is the first goal, the evaluation is finished.

Fig. 3.3 Depth-first search procedure for solving goal statements.

goal statement like

```
x plays y  &  y plays x
```

it is easy to see that the outcome is failure, just by inspecting the two goals. Alas, PROLOG does not have this much intelligence and it will use a depth-first search every time.

Practical points

We pointed out earlier that the order in which goals appear in a conjunction should not affect the outcome of an evaluation. In reality however, two considerations have to be borne in mind.

First, the order often makes a difference to the **efficiency** of PROLOG's evaluation. As an example, to solve the problem: 'Does anyone play squash and Ian play tennis?', we could try the query

```
is(x plays squash  &  Ian plays tennis)
```

or alternatively, we could try

```
is(Ian plays tennis  &  x plays squash)
```

Both queries will be correctly answered `NO`, but the second query will be answered more quickly because the failure of its first goal `Ian plays tennis` will result in the failure of the whole goal statement immediately. The other query will cause PROLOG, following the depth-first strategy, to try every solution to `x plays squash` before conceding that none of them can make a success of `Ian plays tennis`. With a small database of facts like SPORT, this inefficiency does not matter; but in some problems efficiency will be a concern.

Second, the order in which we write goals in a conjunction can influence the outcome if the goals involve negations or relations with special restrictions. This will be easier to understand when we have looked at the built-in relations (Chapter 4), but we can illustrate the problem of negations now with a small example. To solve the problem: 'Which game does Tony play which is not played with a bat?', we could try the query

```
which(x :  Tony plays x  &  not x played-with bat)
```

which will be answered correctly. But it would be wrong to use the alternative ordering of goals:

```
which(x :  not x played-with bat  &  Tony plays x)
```

and this query will **not** produce the answers. The reason is that with this query PROLOG's depth-first strategy will try to solve `not x played-with bat` first: but a negation, as we saw earlier, cannot be used to generate answers. In the first query the negation is only being used to test, since by the time it is evaluated `x` will have been replaced by a term.

Exercise

Evaluate mentally the following goal statements using the SPORT database, writing either 'succeeds' or 'fails' for each one. Where a goal statement succeeds, state any replacements for variables. Then by forming suitable queries check that PROLOG's answers agree with yours.

(a) `x played-with bases`
(b) `y plays soccer`
(c) `Alison plays x`
(d) `tennis played-with ball`
(e) `Tony plays tennis`
(f) `hockey played-with z`
(g) `squash played-with x & baseball played-with x`
(h) `x played-with racket & y plays x`
(i) `Helen plays x & x played-with y`
(j) `Y plays tennis & Y plays baseball`
(k) `x1 played-with x2 & Ian plays x1`
(l) `not George plays squash`
(m) `Tony plays x & not Alison plays x`

Construct diagrams similar to Figure 3.2 corresponding to PROLOG's evaluation of these goal statements:

(n) `Alison plays x & x played-with y`
(o) `x plays squash & squash played-with y`
(p) `z played-with ball & x plays z`
(q) `Tony plays x & y plays x`

EVALUATING GOALS WITH RULES

Facts, as we have seen, can solve problems (goals) at once. Rules on the other hand cannot. A rule transforms a problem into other problems. The hope is always that these 'other' problems will be solvable, perhaps through the use of further rules, but ultimately by using facts.

You may be wondering how a rule can help in solving a problem at all. The answer lies in the idea that every rule, as well as being a statement of logic, can also be viewed as a **problem-solving procedure**. As a simple illustration of this, consider the sentence of English:

> Any friend of Diane's who enjoys reggae
> is invited to Sam's party.

We can read this sentence in two different ways. First, it can be interpreted as a statement of logic with a consequence part and a condition part, like this:

> Someone is invited to Sam's party if
> they are a friend of Diane's and
> they enjoy reggae.

This is the usual **logical interpretation** of the sentence. But the sentence can also be viewed as a procedure which shows how an invitation to Sam's party can be obtained:

> To be invited to Sam's party:
> (1) Become friendly with Diane and
> (2) Develop a taste for reggae.

This **procedural interpretation** of the sentence is very useful. It shows how the problem of being invited to Sam's party can be solved, by transforming the problem into two other problems concerned with being a friend of Diane and enjoying reggae. If we can solve these two other problems, the original problem will have been solved.

PROLOG makes use of database rules to solve problems exactly like this. Each rule is given a procedural interpretation which shows how certain kinds of goals can be solved. In what follows, we look at this more fully.

Some examples

Formally, we say that a rule **applies** to a goal if the goal can be made identical to the head of an instance of the rule. PROLOG then evaluates the goal by selecting the **tail of the instance of the rule** as the new goal statement.

The concept of the **instances** of a rule is one which we met in the last chapter. Essentially, the idea is that a rule is not changed by re-naming its variables, and replacing any variable throughout the rule by a term just gives a special case of the rule. Any such rule obtained by this process is called an instance of the original rule. For example, consider the rule

```
x kind-to y if x likes y
```

Among the instances of the rule are the following:

```
Sally kind-to y if Sally likes y
x kind-to Henry if x likes Henry
Dracula kind-to piglet if Dracula likes piglet
z kind-to Attila-the-Hun if z likes Attila-the-Hun
```

and so on.

Now we shall consider some examples of applying rules to goals.

(a) GOAL: `Henry late`
RULE: `Henry late if car faulty`

The goal is identical to the head of the rule, and so the rule does apply. PROLOG interprets the rule as a procedure which says

To solve the goal `Henry late,`
solve `car faulty.`

NEW GOAL: `car faulty`

(b) GOAL: `sparrow has feathers`
RULE: `x has feathers if x type-of bird`

One instance of the rule is:

```
sparrow has feathers if sparrow type-of bird
```

the head of which is identical to the goal. Hence the rule applies to the goal. PROLOG will find this matching instance and will interpret it as a procedure which says

> To solve the goal `sparrow has feathers`,
> solve `sparrow type-of bird`.

NEW GOAL: `sparrow type-of bird`

(c) GOAL: `z retires`
RULE: `x retires if x age 65`

The rule is equivalent to

```
z retires if z age 65
```

the head of which is identical to the goal. As above, PROLOG selects the tail of this rule as the new goal.

NEW GOAL: `z age 65`

(d) GOAL: `Dracula victimizes piglet`
RULE:
```
Dracula victimizes x if
                        x visits Transylvania  &
                        not x carries cross
```

The rule does apply to the goal, because an instance of it is

```
Dracula victimizes piglet if
                        piglet visits Transylvania  &
                        not piglet carries cross
```

the head of which is identical to the goal. The procedural interpretation of this instance gives the new goal statement.

NEW GOAL STATEMENT:
`piglet visits Transylvania & not piglet carries cross.`

(e) GOAL: `butter costs x`
RULE: `fish costs y if sells(z fish y)`

The rule does not apply to the goal, because no instance of the rule can refer to `butter` instead of `fish`. Hence, the rule is of no use in solving this particular problem.

(f) GOAL: `gives(x Mary z)`
RULE: `gives(Santa y1 y2) if`

```
                    y1 asked-for y2  &
                    y1 deserves y2
```

One instance of the rule is

```
gives(Santa Mary z) if
                    Mary asked-for z  &
                    Mary deserves z
```

By making the replacement `x = Santa` in the goal, the goal becomes identical to the head of this instance. Hence the rule applies. PROLOG will make this replacement and will interpret the rule as a procedure which says

> To solve the goal `gives(Santa Mary z)`,
> solve the goal statement
> `Mary asked-for z & Mary deserves z.`

If this new goal statement succeeds, the replacement found for `z` will form one half of a solution of which `x = Santa` gives the other half.

NEW GOAL STATEMENT: `Mary asked-for z & Mary deserves z.`

(g) GOAL: `x eats y`
RULE: `y eats meat if y is-carnivore`

Care is needed here, since a variable named `y` appears in both the goal and the rule. These are different variables. An instance of the rule is

```
x eats meat if x is-carnivore
```

and with the replacement `y = meat` in the goal, the goal is made identical to the head of this rule. So the rule applies. As above, the replacement for `y` is half of a possible solution — the other half, giving the corresponding replacement for `x`, will be obtained by solving the new goal.

NEW GOAL: `x is-carnivore`

Exercise

Do the following rules apply to the accompanying goals? If so, then write down the new goal statement which results when the rule is applied to the goal. Make a note of any replacements made to variables in the goal which will contribute part of a possible solution.

(a) GOAL: `George happy`
RULE: `George happy if George studies logic`

(b) GOAL: `Rover barks`
RULE: `x barks if x is-a-dog`

(c) GOAL: `x visits Mary`
RULE:
```
y visits z if
        z ill  &
        y likes z
```

(d) GOAL: `Sally laughs`
RULE:
```
x bleeds if
        x is-human  &
        y cuts x
```

(e) GOAL: `x lives-in y`
RULE: `z lives-in water if z type-of fish`

(f) GOAL: `sends(Dibble Alison x)`
RULE:
```
sends(x Alison bicycle) if
        x friend-of Alison  &
        x owns bicycle
```

Alternative rules

Each of the three rules

```
x safe-from Dracula if x carries cross
x safe-from Dracula if x dead
x safe-from Dracula if x stays-in London
```

describes a condition which ensures that an individual is safe from Dracula. Each rule makes sense independently of the other rules, but taken together we can suppose that they form a complete definition of the `safe-from` relation.

PROLOG interprets such alternative rules for the same relation as **alternative problem-solving procedures**. The rules will be applied to solve goals in the same order as they occur in the database. For instance, to solve the goal

```
Sally safe-from Dracula
```

PROLOG will first apply the top rule, obtaining the new goal

```
Sally carries cross
```

If and when this fails, PROLOG will next apply the second rule to form the new goal

```
Sally dead
```

failing which the last hope is obtained by applying the third rule

```
Sally stays-in London
```

Only if all three of these fail does the goal `Sally safe-from Dracula` fail.

Notice in passing that in English, it would be most natural to express the three `safe-from` rules in the form of a single sentence in which the word 'or' connects the conditions.(4) That is, we would say something like

> Someone is safe from Dracula if they carry a cross, or they are dead, or they stay in London.

In PROLOG we must write one sentence to describe each case. Although this is more long-winded, it does have the advantage that it is usually easier to understand several simple sentences than one complicated one; and sentences which are easy to understand are more likely to correspond to correct descriptions.

TRACING EVALUATION

We can now draw together all of the above and consider some full goal evaluations, using a database which includes both facts and rules.

To serve as a source of examples, Figure 3.4 shows the FRONT-ROW database. The database contains a description of the scene

```
Jill left-of Bob                                   (1)
Bob left-of Tony                                   (2)
Tony left-of Tracey                                (3)
Tracey left-of Ian                                 (4)
Ian left-of Mary                                   (5)
Mary left-of Sam                                   (6)

Jill mutters                                       (7)
Mary mutters                                       (8)

Bob cheers                                         (9)
Tracey cheers                                      (10)
Ian cheers                                         (11)

Tony dozes                                         (12)
Sam dozes                                          (13)

x beside y if x left-of y                          (14)
x beside y if y left-of x                          (15)

x happy if x cheers                                (16)

x disturbed-by y if                                (17)
                   x dozes  &
                   x beside y  &
                   y cheers
```

Fig. 3.4 FRONT-ROW.

presented by a group of friends at a soccer match (see Figure 3.5). Sentences 1–13 are facts which declare the relative seating positions

Fig. 3.5

and the activities of the individuals; sentences 14 and 15 are rules which taken together define the `beside` relation; sentence 16 defines the `happy` relation, and sentence 17 declares that individuals who doze are disturbed by cheering neighbors.

Logic trace notation

To represent PROLOG's procedure for evaluating goals we shall use **logic trace notation**, which is a more convenient notation than the one we used earlier in Figure 3.2. The best way to understand logic trace notation is to study a few examples. Follow each one through, referring to the FRONT-ROW database as you go. After each example you might like to make up a query to check that PROLOG gives the same answers as those discovered by the trace.

To assist with explanation, each of the examples below has lines which are labelled with a letter.

(1) Figure 3.6

(a) The goal is `x happy`.

(b) Starting from the top of the database, the first matching sentence is the rule at sentence 16. Applying the rule to the goal makes `x cheers` the new goal. (Read the '`<--`' as meaning 'is satisfied by'.)

(c) Starting from the top of the database, this new goal is first satisfied by `x = Bob` using the fact at sentence 9,

(d) ... and again by `x = Tracey` at sentence 10,

(e) ... and again by `x = Ian` at sentence 11,

(f) ... but by no other sentence. (Notice how the vertical alignment of arrows shows which goal is the current goal.)

(g) So PROLOG asks: 'Is there an alternative sentence matching `x happy`, below sentence 16 where the goal last succeeded?'. There is not.

(h) The evaluation is complete.

```
GOAL: x happy                                   (a)
        <-- x cheers (16)                       (b)
            <-- x = Bob (9)                     (c)
            <-- x = Tracey (10)                 (d)
            <-- x = Ian (11)                    (e)
            <-- ?                               (f)
        <-- ?                                   (g)
No (more) answers                               (h)
```

Fig. 3.6

(2) Figure 3.7

(a) The goal this time is `x beside Bob`.

(b) The first matching sentence is sentence 14, which is a rule which makes `x left-of Bob` the new goal.

(c) Sentence 1 solves this with `x = Jill`,

(d) ... but no other matching sentence is found.

(e) So PROLOG asks: 'Is there an alternative sentence, one below sentence 14, which matches `x beside Bob`?'. The alternative rule at sentence 15 is discovered which makes the new goal `Bob left-of x`,

(f) — and sentence 2 gives `x = Tony` as a solution to this.

(g) But no other matching sentence is found.

(h) Nor are there any alternative sentences to match `x beside Bob` below sentence 15 (where it last succeeded), and so the evaluation ends.

```
GOAL: x beside Bob                                   (a)
      <-- x left-of Bob   (14)                       (b)
          <-- x = Jill   (1)                         (c)
          <-- ?                                      (d)
      <-- Bob left-of x   (15)                       (e)
          <-- x = Tony   (2)                         (f)
          <-- ?                                      (g)
      <-- ?                                          (h)
No (more) answers
```

Fig. 3.7

(3) Figure 3.8

(a) The goal is the negation `not Jill mutters`.

(b) To evaluate it, PROLOG selects `Jill mutters` as the goal (notice how it is enclosed in curly brackets to show that its evaluation is a 'by-product' of evaluating the negation).

(c) This goal succeeds, by sentence 7

(d) — and so the negation fails.

```
GOAL: not Jill mutters                               (a)
      {Jill mutters                                  (b)
       <--   (7)}                                    (c)
      <-- ?                                          (d)
No (more) answers
```

Fig. 3.8

(4) Figure 3.9

(a) The goal statement is `x mutters & x left-of y`.

(b) The depth-first strategy selects `x mutters` as the first goal

(c) ... and it succeeds with `x = Jill` at sentence 7

(d) — so PROLOG forward-tracks with this replacement. The second goal now becomes `Jill left-of y`

(e) ... which succeeds with `y = Bob` at sentence 1 (making `x = Jill`, `y = Bob` a solution to the original goal statement)

(f) ... but no other sentence matches it.

(g) PROLOG back-tracks. The replacement `x = Jill` is abandoned, and a solution to `x mutters` below sentence 7 is sought. `x = Mary` is found using sentence 8.

(h) Forward-tracking with this replacement, the second goal `x left-of y` now becomes `Mary left-of y`

(i) ... and `y = Sam` solves this goal by sentence 6 (`x = Mary`, `y = Sam` now gives a second solution to the goal statement)

(j) ... but no other sentence matches it.

(k) Back-tracking, the attempt to find a match for `x mutters` below sentence 8 fails. The evaluation ends.

GOAL STATEMENT:	x mutters	&	x left-of y		(a)
	x mutters				(b)
	<-- x = Jill	(7)			(c)
			Jill left-of y		(d)
			<-- y = Bob	(1)	(e)
			<-- ?		(f)
	<-- x = Mary	(8)			(g)
			Mary left-of y		(h)
			<-- y = Sam	(6)	(i)
			<-- ?		(j)
	<-- ?				(k)
No (more) answers					

Fig. 3.9

(5) Figure 3.10

(a) The goal is `Tony disturbed-by x`.

(b) Applying sentence 17 gives a goal statement with three conditions

(c) — of which the first goal succeeds by sentence 12.

(d) Forward-tracking, sentence 14 applies to the second goal to make the new goal `Tony left-of x`

(e) ... which is solved by `x = Tracey` using sentence 3.

(f) Forward-tracking again, the third goal with this replacement is solved by sentence 10 (making `x = Tracey` a solution to the original goal)

```
GOAL: Tony disturbed-by x                                              (a)
      <-- Tony dozes    &    Tony beside x    &    x cheers (17)(b)
          Tony dozes
          <--  (12)                                                    (c)
                          Tony beside x
                          <-- Tony left-of x   (14)                    (d)
                              <-- x = Tracey   (3)                     (e)
                                               Tracey cheers
                                               <--   (10)   (f)
                                               <-- ?        (g)
                              <-- ?                                    (h)
                          <-- x left-of Tony   (15)                    (i)
                              <-- x = Bob   (2)                        (j)
                                               Bob cheers
                                               <--   (9)    (k)
                                               <-- ?        (l)
                              <-- ?                                    (m)
                          <-- ?
          <-- ?
      <-- ?
No (more) answers
```

Fig. 3.10

(g) — but no other sentence applies.

(h) `Tony left-of x` finds no alternative solution on back-tracking.

(i) ... but `Tony beside x` is matched by sentence 15. This alternative `beside` rule gives the new goal `x left-of Tony`

(j) — which `x = Bob` solves,

(k) — and `Bob cheers` is proved by sentence 9. This gives a second solution to the original goal.

(l) No other sentence applies to `Bob cheers`.

(m) PROLOG back-tracks through all the previous goals. But none of them are matched by further sentences and the evaluation ends.

Tracing goals with SIMTRACE

Tracing goal evaluations by hand is hard work. Fortunately, it's a job which a computer can do on our behalf. SIMTRACE is a program provided with the PROLOG package which will trace goals automatically.

To trace the goal shown in Figure 3.6 (say) using SIMTRACE, you must first load SIMTRACE into your computer's memory. This is done with the command

```
load SIMTRACE
```

Then, with FRONT-ROW as the current database, enter

```
all-trace(x : x happy)
```

`all-trace` is a form of query very like `which`, except that SIMTRACE takes you through the evaluation step by step (you can skip parts of it by responding `n` instead of `y` to the prompt `trace ?` if you wish). It's a good idea to follow it through with Figure 3.6 in front of you, so that you can compare SIMTRACE's output with the logic trace notation version. Note however that SIMTRACE re-names the variables in each condition it traces, using the same scheme as PROLOG applies to re-name variables in database sentences.

SIMTRACE takes up room in your computer's memory, so when

you have finished with it enter the command

```
kill simtrace-mod
```

to free the memory space again. (The 'mod' is used because SIMTRACE is a so-called 'module' — a PROLOG program which has been packaged-up so that it becomes an extension to the PROLOG system when in use.)[(5)]

SIMTRACE is a very useful tool, but it has disadvantages. The screen tends to flood with information which can be more confusing than helpful. An evaluation written by hand, with its 'pretty' layout, sometimes gives a more useful picture of events.

Exercise

Using logic trace notation, trace the evaluation of each of the following goal statements using the FRONT-ROW database. If possible, use SIMTRACE to check that your answer is correct.

(a) `Tony dozes`
(b) `Mary beside z`
(c) `Jill happy`
(d) `x dozes & y left-of x`
(e) `not Bob cheers`
(f) `x happy & x beside Mary`
(g) `x disturbed-by Bob`

FLOW DIAGRAMS

An important feature of PROLOG is that the same database sentence (or sentences) can often be used to solve a variety of different types of problem. We say that the sentences which define a relation are **invertible** in the way in which they can be used.

To illustrate, consider the sentence

```
gives(x y z) if
            x likes y &
            y deserves z
```

Assuming that the `likes` and `deserves` relations are suitably defined, we can use this sentence to solve goals of various types. For instance,

(a) We can supply the name of an individual and seek a corresponding 'giver' and 'thing given', as in the goal

```
gives(X Mary Z)
```

(b) We can supply the names of an individual and an object, and seek a corresponding recipient, as exemplified by

```
gives(Santa X bicycle)
```

(c) We can supply the names of two individuals and an object, and determine whether the relationship holds between them. An example is

```
gives(Dad John Honda)
```

(d) We can ask which individuals and objects have the relationship, for instance with the goal

```
gives(X1 X2 X3)
```

And so on. In each case, certain of the three arguments are supplied (`Mary`, `Honda`, etc.): these are called the **goal inputs**. The remaining arguments are variables for which PROLOG is expected to find suitable replacements: these are known as **goal outputs**.

In theory, any combination of the arguments of a relation can be goal inputs, with the others as goal outputs. Fixing on a particular input/output combination gives a particular type of goal for that relation. For example, the goals

```
gives(X Moses Z)
gives(y Fred z)
gives(y1 Dracula y2)
```

are all goals for the `gives` relation of the same type as (a) above, in that the first and third arguments are goal outputs and the second is a goal input in each case.

A **flow diagram** is a picture which shows which of a relation's arguments are inputs and which are outputs in a particular type of goal for the relation. Figures 3.11 (a)–(d) are flow diagrams for the types of goals represented by (a)–(d) above. As you can see, the goal itself appears inside a circle with variables to represent the argu-

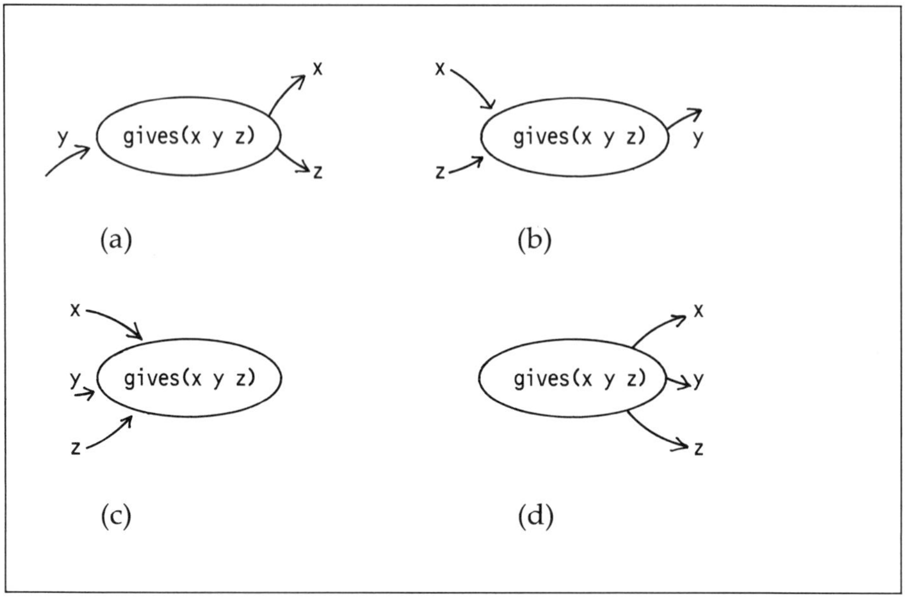

Fig. 3.11

ments; those which are inputs are shown entering from the left and outputs are shown exiting from the right.

Notice that a flow diagram assumes that the goal which it represents will succeed. If the goal fails, then no replacements for variables are made and the diagram does not apply. For example, should `X likes Mary` fail (say, because nobody exists who likes Mary) then the goal `gives(X Mary Z)` fails with the above rule, and so Figure 3.11 (a) does not present a correct picture.

Flow diagrams are very useful for depicting the procedural interpretation of a rule. For instance, the flow diagram in Figure 3.12 illustrates how a goal of the type `gives(X Mary Z)` could be solved using the rule above. Applying the rule to the goal will result in the new goal statement

```
X likes Mary  &  Mary deserves Z
```

so that PROLOG will first try to solve a `likes` goal in which the first argument is an output and the second an input, and then a `deserves` goal in which the first argument is an input and the second is an output. Hence, Figure 3.12 shows flow diagrams for these types of goals in sequence, both contained inside a flow diagram corresponding to the type of the original `gives` goal.

This kind of flow diagram provides a useful check. It shows the flow of inputs and outputs through a particular use of a rule in such a way as to make any inconsistencies — such as inputs which arise from nowhere — easy to spot. Such diagrams are also useful in designing programs, as we shall discover later.

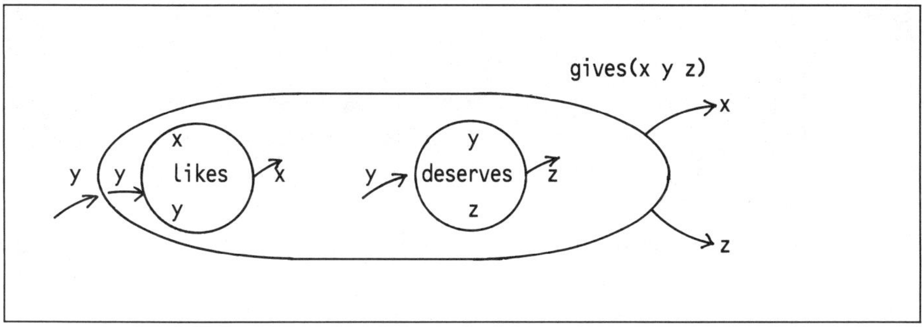

Fig. 3.12

SUMMARY

(1) A goal is a problem to be solved, represented by an atom or a negation. An evaluation of a goal either succeeds (possibly with replacements) or fails.

(2) A conjunction of goals (called a goal statement) is evaluated using the depth-first strategy, in which goals are evaluated from left to right. When a goal succeeds, the replacements are carried forward; when a goal fails, PROLOG back-tracks for alternatives.

(3) A goal succeeds if

— it can be made identical to a fact, or
— a rule applies to the goal, and the resulting goal statement succeeds, or
— it is a negation, and the corresponding atom fails as a goal.

When looking for sentences which match a goal, PROLOG examines the database from the top downwards.

(4) Evaluations can be traced by hand using logic trace notation or automatically using the SIMTRACE program.

(5) Flow diagrams can be used to show which arguments of a relation are inputs and which are outputs in a particular type of goal for the relation.

NOTES

(1) And if the PROLOG had come back with the names of non-golfers, say `Jane-Fonda`, `Bruce-Lee`, `Prince-Charles`, ... then that **would** have been something!

(2) Parallel processing is one of the main targets of fifth generation project workers. The Japanese for example plan to build by 1990 PROLOG computers which exploit parallel processing to give astounding evaluation speeds of over one hundred million logical deductions per second (micro-PROLOG does around 240).

(3) The name refers to the way in which PROLOG investigates the solution to the first goal as 'deeply' as possible before trying an alternative to it.

(4) The technical term is a **disjunction** of conditions.

(5) Unfortunately, on computers with small usable memory SIMTRACE will quickly run out of memory space. SIMTRACE is of limited use on these machines.

4 A toolkit for description

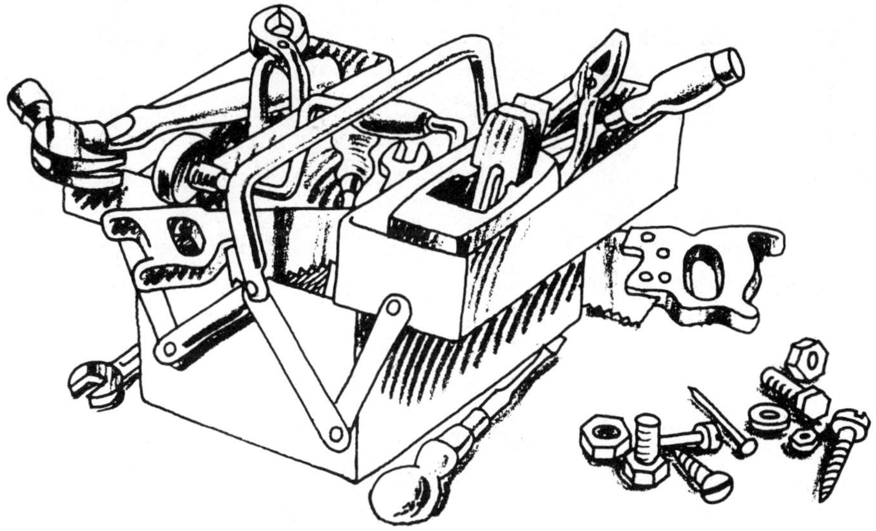

In this chapter we look at some of the built-in relations of micro-PROLOG. Together they comprise a kind of resident PROLOG toolkit, always available to help with the work of writing descriptions. The built-in relations are a permanent feature of the system; you don't have to add them to your databases, nor load them into memory from disk or tape.

SUM

The SUM relation is used for addition and subtraction. A SUM goal has three arguments, and it will succeed if PROLOG can make replacements such that the third argument is the total of the other two. Try a few examples, like these:

```
which(x :  SUM(2 3 x))   which(x :  SUM(6 x 14))   is(SUM(5.3 3.2 8.5))
5                        8                         YES
No (more) answers        No (more) answers
```

SUM is invertible, as you can see. But it does have one important restriction: at least two of its arguments must be inputs. If you break this rule, say by a query such as

```
which(x y :  SUM(x y 10))
```

then PROLOG will complain with an error message. This restriction on **SUM** is unfortunate. Ideally, PROLOG should respond to a query like the one above by displaying pairs of numbers which add up to ten. This is what would happen if **SUM** was defined by a large database of addition facts, for example. Instead, PROLOG relies on being given enough inputs to ensure that a single calculation will suffice to evaluate any **SUM** goal.(1)

We can immediately use **SUM** to define some further relations. For example

```
x one-less-than y if SUM(x 1 y)
x one-more-than y if SUM(y 1 x)
```

Even though these rules have only one condition, the relations they define are useful; they can help to make the definitions of further relations easier to understand than if we always inserted a bare **SUM** relation instead. But notice that the limitations on **SUM** affects these new relations too; the query

```
which(x y :  x one-less-than y)
```

for example produces an error message because it results in a **SUM** goal with too few inputs.

TIMES

TIMES is the multiplication and division relation. A few examples show that **TIMES** behaves in a way similar to **SUM**:

```
which(x :  TIMES(3 5 x))
15
No (more) answers
```

```
which(x :  TIMES(x -25 92.5))
-3.7
No (more) answers
```

```
is(TIMES(3.4 8.7 29.58))
YES
```

`TIMES` has the same restriction as `SUM` in that at least two arguments of a goal for the relation must be inputs.

Some numbers, for example very large numbers, are displayed by micro-PROLOG in a special form which is known as **standard form**. Try a query like

```
which(x : TIMES(1000000 1000000 x))
1.0E12
No (more) answers
```

The answer 1.0E12 is equivalent to 1.0×10^{12}, or 1000000000000 in ordinary notation.

INT

`x INT` is true if `x` is an integer. Hence `125 INT` is true and `27.3 INT` is false. The argument of an `INT` goal must be an input: the relation cannot be used to **generate** integers.

We can use `INT` and `TIMES` together to define a useful relationship `x factor-of y`, which holds when `x` is a factor (that is, an integral divisor) of `y`. We shall assume that `x` and `y` are both integers. The definition is

```
x factor-of y if
                TIMES(x z y)  &
                z INT
```

Figure 4.1 shows how a `factor-of` goal can check that two inputs have the relationship. Actually, this is the only legal type of `factor-of` goal — if you try to draw a flow diagram for any other type you will come up against the restrictions on `TIMES` and `INT`.

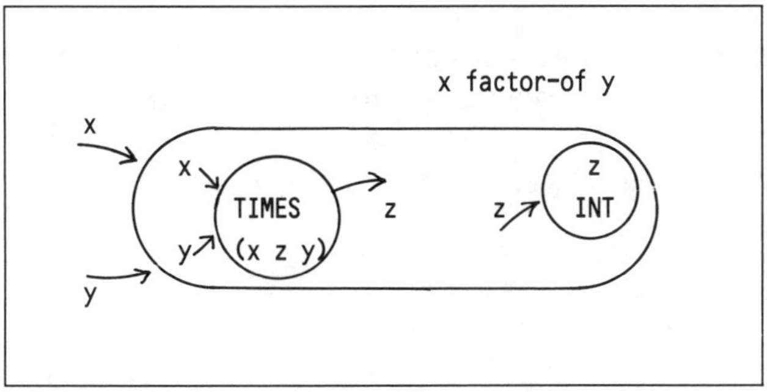

Fig. 4.1

There is a second, two-argument form of INT which is used for rounding to whole numbers. In this form, the first argument must be a number and the second a variable. An INT goal of this type will succeed by replacing the variable by the integral part of the number. For example, the goal

```
2.3 INT y
```

will succeed and will result in the replacement y=2.

LESS

x LESS y is true if x is a number smaller than the number y. The relation can only be used for checking purposes — that is, both arguments must be inputs.

PROLOG does not have a corresponding built-in greater-than relation, but it is an easy matter to define one of our own:

```
x greater-than y if y LESS x
```

Again, the restriction on LESS means that greater-than can only be used for checking.

EQ

x EQ y is true if x and y are identical terms. Examples are

```
is(2 EQ 2)    is(23 EQ 32)    is(Carol EQ Diane)
YES           NO              NO
```

If an EQ goal is supplied with only one input, the goal will succeed by making an identical replacement for the other argument. For instance

```
which(x : x EQ treacle)          which(y : 123.4 EQ y)
treacle                          123.4
No (more) answers                No (more) answers
```

A useful arithmetic relationship is x lessoreq y, which holds when x and y are numbers with x less than or equal to y. One way to define lessoreq is to write the following two rules:

```
x lessoreq y if x LESS y
x lessoreq y if x EQ y
```

Because of the restriction on LESS, it is safe to use lessoreq only for checking that two numbers have the relationship. Try a few examples:

```
is(3 lessoreq 8)        is(1 lessoreq -2.5)      is(100 lessoreq 100)
YES                     NO                       YES
```

P AND PP

P (Print) and PP (Pretty Print) are not really 'relations' at all. They are procedures which tell PROLOG to display their arguments on the screen.

Normally, the answers to queries are the only kind of screen display we require. There are however occasions when we need something extra and it is at these times that P and PP come into play. Both P and PP can take any number of arguments, which will be printed on the screen in left-to-right order. If any of the arguments are replaced variables, then it is the replacements for the variables which will be displayed.

The main difference betweeen P and PP is that PP moves to a new line after printing, whereas P does not. Here are some examples:

```
is(P(Hi there folks))   is(PP(Hi there folks))  is(x EQ 2  &  PP(x))
Hi there folksYES       Hi there folks          2
                        YES                     YES
```

Of course, these are not really 'queries' at all — they are simply a means of letting us see the effect of PROLOG's evaluation of a Print goal. Actually PROLOG always regards such a goal as succeeding (hence the YES answers) but the effect we are really after is the printing of the arguments on the screen.

One important use for P and PP is in the provision of **trace points**. A trace point is a Print goal which is used for fault-finding: the idea is to insert it into a rule or goal statement so as to provide information about what happens during evaluation. Suppose for example that we were interested in PROLOG's evaluation of the goal statement

```
x beside y  &  y dozes
```

using the FRONT-ROW database from page 51. A useful query could be

```
which(x y :  x beside y  &  PP(Trying x and y)  &  y dozes)
```

The second goal here is a trace point. It will not affect the answers to the query in any way (Print goals always succeed, remember) but it will cause replacements for x and y to be displayed as they are tried. Trace points, alongside logic tracing by hand and with SIMTRACE, are a useful tool for tackling faults in (or 'debugging') PROLOG programs.

R

Like P and PP, R (Read) is a 'relation' which is actually a procedure. It tells PROLOG to read something from the keyboard. An R goal has a single argument, which must be a variable, and its effect is to read a term which is typed at the keyboard and make that term a replacement for the variable. To indicate that some keyboard input is expected, PROLOG will display its '.' prompt. The term entered can be a number, a word or a list (the brackets of a list must be typed). Whatever the term happens to be, PROLOG always regards an R goal as having succeeded.

As an example, suppose that we are writing a program which required the age of the user to be entered during a program run. A sentence which might help is

```
x is-age if
          P(How old are you?)  &
          R(x)
```

PROLOG will interpret this rule as a procedure which says: 'To solve the goal x is-age, Print the question on the screen and Read x as the user's answer'. A suitable query will show you what it does:

```
which(x :  x is-age)
How old are you?.17
17
No (more) answers
```

(The first 17 was typed at the keyboard.) Try it and see for yourself!

Exercise

Write down the outcome of the following goal statements as either success or failure. If the goal statement succeeds, write down any replacements for its variables.

(a) `SUM(3 -4 y)`
(b) `TIMES(2 6 3)`
(c) `3 LESS 4`
(d) `SUM(2 4 x)  &  TIMES(x 5 y)`
(e) `-52 INT`
(f) `TIMES(z 5 194)  &  z INT`
(g) `SUM(5 X 9)  &  TIMES(X X Z)  &  Z LESS 16`
(h) `4.6 INT z  &  TIMES(z x z)`
(i) `tomato EQ y`

TWO COMMENTS ON EVALUATION

(1) The restrictions on the use of the built-in relations means that we must be especially careful about the positioning of these relations in goal statements and rules. To illustrate, consider the problem: 'Which number is five times more than a number which is three less than 10?'. Using the query

```
which(x :  SUM(3 y 10)  &  TIMES(y 5 x))
```

PROLOG solves the problem correctly, whereas the alternative query in which the goals are re-ordered:

```
which(x :  TIMES(y 5 x)  &  SUM(3 y 10))
```

produces only an error message. The explanation is that

PROLOG evaluates the left goal first, and in the second query this goal has fewer inputs than is allowed by the restriction on `TIMES`. In the first query, `y` is a replaced variable in the `TIMES` goal (the success of `SUM` replaces the variable with a number) and the error does not occur.

(2) A goal for a built-in relation will succeed in **at most one way**. That is, PROLOG does not attempt to re-satisfy it on backtracking. If this were not the case, for instance, then a query such as

```
is(PP(pigs can fly) & SUM(2 2 5))
```

would cause `pigs can fly` to be printed on the screen over and over again!

SUMMARY

Table 4.1 summarizes the main points about the built-in relations which have been covered in this chapter.

Table 4.1

RELATION	EXAMPLE	MAIN USE
SUM	SUM(3 4 x)	Addition and subtraction
TIMES	TIMES(6 x 42)	Multiplication and division
INT	23 INT	Checking that a number is an integer
	4.6 INT z	Finding the integer part of a number
LESS	x LESS 12	Checking order
EQ	x1 EQ x2	Checking equality
P, PP	P(Enter a number)	Printing terms on screen
R	R(x)	Reading terms from keyboard

NOTE

(1) The root cause of the restriction on `SUM` is the lack of computing power provided by current microprocessors. Micro-PROLOG's developers have compromised with most of the built-in relations, making them as invertible as possible given the limitations of the underlying hardware.

5 Representing objects

The PROLOG sentences — facts and rules — which we have come across so far have mainly described relationships between quite simple objects, such as the names of individuals, varieties of games, kinds of music and so on. Objects like these are easily represented in a form suitable for PROLOG by using terms such as `Diane`, `football`, and `heavy-metal`, each of which PROLOG recognizes as a word. But the task of representing objects is not always this easy. Some objects are complex. Consider for example a person's entry in a telephone book; or the state of a chessboard in mid-play; or the collection of raffle tickets held by an individual. These are all examples of objects which figure in real problems, but none of them could readily be represented by a single word. Fortunately, PROLOG has another kind of term: **lists**. So far we haven't seen much of them. In this chapter we shall discover that lists are the key to representing more complex objects in PROLOG.

ABOUT LISTS

A list is a bracketed sequence of terms which are known as its **members**. The members may be terms of any type: numbers, words, variables or lists. So each of these is a list:

```
(pies eggs chips beans)
((Mary Jones) (23 New St Eastham) (28 29228))
(201 463 76 603 700 388)
(x1 y1)
(pawn x 5)
```

The first list here is a list of four members, all of which are words. The second list has three members, all lists; the third has six members, all numbers; the fourth contains two members, both of which are variables; and the fifth contains three members — a word, a variable and a number. The order in which members appear within a list matters: so a list is not the same thing as a **set** in mathematics, for example.

Lists can be 'nested', if necessary, to any depth. An example is

```
(this (is (a (list) ) ) )
```

which is a list containing two members, the first being the word `this` and the second being the list `(is (a (list) ) )`, which itself has two members. (The spaces beside the brackets here aren't needed — they are only to make the structure of the list easier to see.) Notice that list brackets occur in matched pairs, just as they do in algebraic expressions (and in (correctly) written English!).

Lists appear in PROLOG sentences as the arguments of relations. For example, we might find these sentences in a database:

```
George eats (pies eggs chips beans)                        (1)
((Mary Jones) (23 New St Eastham) (28 29228))  is-entry    (2)
Diane holds-tickets (201 463 76 603 700 388)               (3)
(x1 y1) reflects-to (x1 y2) if y2 negative-of y1           (4)
```

In passing, notice that sentences like these show the naturalness of the infix and postfix atomic forms. The same sentences could have been written equivalently in prefix as

```
eats(George  (pies eggs chips beans))
is-entry(((Mary Jones) (23 New St Eastham) (28 29228)))
holds-tickets(Diane  (201 463 76 603 700 388))
reflects-to((x1 y1) (x1 y2)) if negative-of(y2 y1)
```

but these versions are much more awkward to read.

Lists provide a way of representing the structure which occurs in a complex object. For instance, an individual's telephone entry can be considered as having three distinct components, and so the example above represented an entry as a list with the structure

```
((NAME) (ADDRESS) (NUMBER))
```

Since a list is a kind of term, and since any term can be represented by a variable, we can 'get at' the parts of a list by using variables to represent the members. Consider these queries for example, using sentences 1–4 above:

```
which(x :  George eats x)
(pies eggs chips beans)
No (more) answers

which (x :  x is-entry)
((Mary Jones) (23 New St Eastham) (28 29228))
No (more) answers

which(x : ((Mary Jones) y x) is-entry)
(28 29228)
No (more) answers

which(x :  (y x (28 29228)) is-entry)
(23 New St Eastham)
No (more) answers

which(x :  Diane holds-tickets (x y2 y3 y4 y5 y6))
201
No (more) answers
```

PROLOG answered each query by finding replacement terms for the variables in the query goal which made the goal identical to a fact in the database. Notice that this is possible only in the case of list arguments if the numbers of members in the lists are equal, and if corresponding members which are non-variables are identical. For instance, the lists `(y x (28 29228))` and `((Mary Jones) (23 New St Eastham) (28 29228))` are made identical by making the replacements `y = (Mary Jones)`, `x = (23 New St Eastham)`, but a pair of lists such as `(pies eggs chips beans)` and `(x y z)` can never be made identical since the second list will always have only three members no matter how the variables are replaced.[1]

A question of terminology arises here. By what name can we refer to terms which appear inside list arguments of relations — for instance, the term `pies` in sentence 1 above? It is **not** an argument (the `eats` relation has two arguments, and here `George` is one and `(pies eggs chips beans)` is the other). For this reason we introduce the word **parameter**. The parameters of a relation are its arguments, plus all the terms which appear at any level within the list arguments. So the parameters of

```
George eats (pies eggs chips beans)
```

are

```
George
(pies eggs chips beans)
pies
eggs
chips
beans
```

Finally, one list deserves a special mention. The list

```
()
```

known as the **empty list** has no members at all. The empty list looks rather dull, but it is actually very useful as we shall find out.

LIST NOTATION

Let us suppose that we have a database containing the fact

```
Diane holds-tickets (201 463 76 603 700 388)
```

as in the last section, but this time along with several thousand others like it. The raffle is drawn, and out of the bag pops ticket number 603. The problem is — who has won? Of course, knowing Diane's tickets as we do, we could easily query

```
which(x : x holds-tickets (y1 y2 y3 603 y5 y6))
```

and get Diane's name back from the computer, but obviously that would be cheating! In general, we couldn't expect to know how many tickets the winner had bought, and nor would we know the position of number 603 within that list. In circumstances like these our method of 'getting at' the members of a list by representing them with variables is not good enough. We need something more powerful.

This is where the **list notation** comes in. In this notation, we consider every list except the empty list as having two parts, called the **head** and the **tail**. The head of a list is the **first member**. The tail is **the list containing all the other members**. The division of a list into the two parts is known as **splitting** the list. Some examples are shown in Table 5.1.

LIST	HEAD	TAIL
(pies eggs beans chips)	pies	(eggs beans chips)
(eggs beans chips)	eggs	(beans chips)
(beans chips)	beans	(chips)
(chips)	chips	()
()	------CANNOT BE SPLIT-------	
(201 463 76 603 700 388)	201	(463 76 603 700 388)
(x1 x2)	x1	(x2)
((A B C) (D E))	(A B C)	((D E))
(this (is (a (list))))	this	((is (a (list))))

Table 5.1

Pictorially, we can represent the two parts of a list like this:

```
(pies  eggs  beans  chips)
  ↑   └--------v---------┘
HEAD        TAIL
```

Be clear that the tail of a list is **always a list**. The head can be a term of any type, depending on what the first member of the list happens to be.

The first four examples in the above table illustrate an important point. If we split a list, and then split the tail, and then split the tail of the tail, and so on, then every member of the list will 'become a head' sooner or later. This is a procedure which lies behind much of what follows in this chapter.

Any list which can be split — that is, any list except the empty list — can be represented by the special pattern

```
(x|Y)
```

in which x stands for the head and Y the tail of the list. (Read the bar as meaning 'followed by', and think of the pattern as a 'picture' which shows the head of the list split apart from the rest.) To illustrate, consider the query

```
which(x Y : Diane holds-tickets (x|Y))
201 (463 76 603 700 388)
No (more) answers
```

The list (x | Y) becomes identical to the list of tickets held by Diane by making the replacements x = 201 (the head of the list) and Y = (463 76 603 700 388) (the tail).

Only the empty list cannot be matched with the pattern (x|Y): every non-empty list can be expressed in this notation. In fact, we could even have entered Diane's list of tickets into the computer in the form (201 | (463 76 603 700 388)) since this is no different from the list (201 463 76 603 700 388).

micro-PROLOG allows the list notation to be used in an extended way. We can write (x1 x2|X) to denote the list in which the first two members are x1 and x2 and the rest of the list is X. Similarly, (x1 x2 x3|X) denotes a list with x1, x2 and x3 as the first three members, and with X as the rest; and so on. Notice however that just as the pattern (x|X) can only represent lists which have at least one member, so (x1 x2|X) and (x1 x2 x3|X) can only represent lists having a minimum of two and three members respectively.

Exercise

Write down replacements for variables which make the following pairs of lists identical (or write 'fails' if this is impossible).

(a) `(1 2 3) and (x 2 3)`
(b) `(1 2 3) and (x y z)`
(c) `(1 2 3) and (1 X 2)`
(d) `(1 2 3) and (Y)`
(e) `(elf eel auk dodo) and (x|Y)`
(f) `(pig cow) and (x|X)`
(g) `(treacle) and (x|X)`
(h) `() and (y|Z)`
(i) `(tall dark handsome Tom) and (tall|X)`
(j) `((1 1) (2 6) (-3 4)) and (x|Y)`
(k) `((Smith married) (Jones single) (Dibble married)) and ((Smith z) |Z)`
(l) `(fee fi fo fum) and (x1 x2 |X)`
(m) `(oo la la tum ti tum) and (x y z |Z)`
(n) `(x y x) and (vampire werewolf piglet)`
(o) `(x y x) and (treacle|(treacle treacle))`

STANDARD LIST RELATIONS

A few relations are in such frequent use in everyday PROLOG work that they have come to be known as the **standard** relations. The standard relations are not (as a rule) built-in: they must be added to the database by the programmer. In this section we consider some standard relations which are useful for working with lists.

`member-of`

The problem we met earlier about which individual's list included the winning raffle ticket is really a problem of **list membership**. What we need is a relation `member-of` such that `x member-of X` is true when `x` is one of the members of a list `X`.

Exercise

Try first to write a definition of the relation for yourself. Represent the list as `(y|Y)`, so that `y` is the head (or first member) and `Y` is the tail (the list of all the other members). Then write one rule which says that x is a member of the list if it is equal to the head, and a second rule which says that x is a member of the list if it is a member of the tail.

Solution

Let us follow the advice given, and spell out the two rules, first in English:

(a) x is a member of (y|Y) if x is equal to y.
(b) x is a member of (y|Y) if x is a member of Y.

Neither of these rules applies to the empty list, but since the empty list doesn't have any members anyway that won't matter. It's easy enough to translate the two rules into PROLOG:

```
x member-of (y|Y) if x EQ y                 (1)
x member-of (y|Y) if x member-of Y          (2)
```

Now we can enter these definitions into a computer. Some queries with which we can try them out are

```
is(3 member-of (2 9 4 3 5))
YES

is(treacle member-of (spam jam tea-leaves))
NO

which(x :  x member-of (fee fi fo fum))
fee
fi
fo
fum
No (more) answers
```

which seems perfect. The question we cannot resist now is — how does it work? Figure 5.1, which shows the start of a logic trace of the goal 3 member-of (2 9 4 3 5), makes the answer clear. PROLOG first applies rule 1 to the goal; a matching instance of the rule for the goal is

```
3 member-of (2 |(9 4 3 5)) if 3 EQ 2
```

but not surprisingly 3 EQ 2 fails. So PROLOG tries the other rule. A matching instance of rule 2 for the goal is

```
3 member-of (2 |(9 4 3 5)) if 3 member-of (9 4 3 5)
```

and so `3 member-of (9 4 3 5)` becomes the new goal. In effect, PROLOG has examined the head of the list to see if it is the required member and, finding it not to be so, it has now begun to examine the tail. And the tail of course is a shorter list (by one member). It's easy to see that after a few more such steps, 3 **will** become the head of the list, and so the goal will succeed by rule 1. If on the other hand 3 **hadn't** been in the list, then eventually the goal would become `3 member-of ()` which would fail (because neither rule applies to the empty list).

```
GOAL: 3 member-of (2 9 4 3 5)
        <-- 3 EQ 2   (1)
            <-- ?
        <-- 3 member-of (9 4 3 5)   (2)
            <-- 3 EQ 9   (1)
                <-- ?
            <-- 3 member-of (4 3 5)   (2)
                ...
```

Fig. 5.1

The relation `member-of` is so useful that it appears in most PROLOG databases. Usually the program[2] appears as

```
x member-of (x|Y)
x member-of (y|Y) if x member-of Y
```

where the first rule here has been abbreviated a little. It has the very same effect as rule 1 above, but pattern-matching does the job of the `EQ` condition.[3]

`length-is`

The length of a list is the number of members which it contains. For example, the length of `(pies eggs chips beans)` is four. A list's length is something we will need to know if we want to find out how many raffle tickets are held by Diane, for example.

Exercise

Try to define a relation `X length-is y` which holds when `y` is the length of a list `X`. As a clue, note that `X` is either empty or non-empty: write one sentence for each case. The length of the empty list is easy. For the non-empty case, write the list as `(z|Z)`, say, and describe its length in terms of the length of `Z` together with a `SUM` condition.

Solution

In English, we can write the two `length-is` sentences as

(a) The empty list has a length of zero.

(b) The list `(z|Z)` has length `y` (say) if `Z` has length `y1` (say) and `y1` plus one is `y`.

Translating this into PROLOG, we get

```
() length-is 0                                  (1)
(z|Z) length-is y if                            (2)
                    Z length-is y1  &
                    SUM(y1 1 y)
```

Now we can try it out with a few queries:

```
is((pies eggs beans chips) length-is 4)
YES

which(x :  (2 9 4 3 5) length-is x)
5
No (more) answers
```

Again, a logic trace will show how it works. The essence of it is this: if the list is non-empty, then the second rule strips the head away and PROLOG begins to find the length of the tail; which, if it is non-empty will result in more head-stripping. Eventually the head-stripping results in the empty list, which the first rule shows to have a fixed length of zero: now all the `SUM`ming of the ones (which goals have been queuing up) can take place. A full logic trace of the goal `(3 5) length-is x` is shown in Figure 5.2. Even though the list here is very short, you can see one of the drawbacks of logic trace notation; as well as being lengthy, traces tend to 'bulge out' in the middle!

```
GOAL: (3 5) length-is x
      <-- (5) length-is y1                          &   SUM(y1 1 x)   (2)

          (5) length-is y1
          <-- () length-is y2 & SUM(y2 1 y1)   (2)

              () length-is y2
              <-- y2=0   (1)
                                  SUM(0  1 y1)
                                  <-- y1=1
                                                    SUM(1  1 x)
                                                    <-- x=2
                                                    <-- ?
                                  <-- ?
              <-- ?
          <-- ?
      <-- ?
No (more) answers
```

Fig. 5.2

An interesting exercise is to re-enter the second `length-is` rule into your computer with the two conditions reversed (that is, put the `SUM` condition first). In strictly logical terms, this shouldn't make any difference: the meaning of a rule is the same no matter in which order the conditions of the rule appear. But if you now try the re-written rule with the same `which`-query as before, you will find that this time you get an error message. Why? The answer lies in the inability of the built-in `SUM` relation to solve `SUM(y1 1 y)`, where `y1` and `y` are both unreplaced variables (with the original ordering, `y1` is a replaced variable). As we remarked on page 69, extra care is needed with the positioning of built-in relations within rules and goal statements.

total-is

A frequent requirement is to find the total of a list of numbers. Let us define a relation `total-is` such that `X total-is y` holds when `y` is the total of the numbers in the number list `X`. For example, `(10 20 30) total-is 60` should be a true relationship.

Exercise

Write the definition. The clue given above for `length-is` applies here too — just replace the word 'length' by 'total' and you have it!

Solution

Two English sentences for `total-is` are

(a) The empty list has a total of zero.
(b) `(z|Z)` has a total of `y` if `Z` has a total of `y1` and `y1` plus `z` equals `y`.

Translating into PROLOG, we get

```
() total-is 0                                        (1)
(z|Z) total-is y if                                  (2)
                Z total-is y1  &
                SUM(y1 z y)
```

The two main uses of this program are shown in the flow diagrams of Figure 5.3, and you should try out a query corresponding to each type of goal.

A useful exercise is to explore exactly how invertible a program really is. Can `total-is` output a list which adds up to a given total, for example? Or can you explain what it does do?

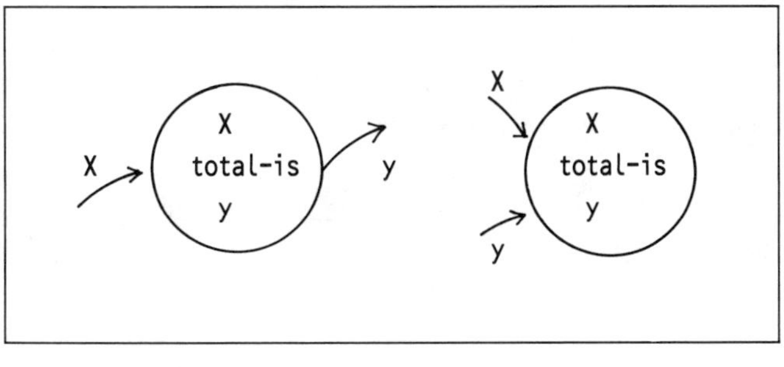

Fig. 5.3

append-to

Suppose for a moment that Carol and Diane, who possess raffle tickets represented by the lists (35 46 301) and (201 463 76 603 700 388) respectively, decide to throw in their lot together. How could we represent the combined stock of tickets? An obvious answer is with the list

```
(35 46 301 201 463 76 603 700 388)
```

where we have simply 'glued' Diane's list on to the end of Carol's. The technical name for this kind of glueing is **appending**. We could describe the appending of the two lists above by writing the relationship

```
((35 46 301) (201 463 76 603 700 388)) append-to
                        (35 46 301 201 463 76 603 700 388)
```

Two other examples are

```
((fe fi fo) (fum)) append-to (fe fi fo fum)
((A B C) (D E)) append-to (A B C D E)
```

Playing with a few examples is a good way to help us think of how the general relationship (X Y) append-to Z might be defined. Consider, for instance, that when we append these two lists

```
(1 2 3)     and     (4 5)
 ↑
```

we get

```
(1 2 3 4 5)
 ↑
```

We have arrowed the head of the result to show where it came from — it came from the head of the first list. This will always be the case. As for the tail of the result, namely the list (2 3 4 5) — from where does that list arise? Somehow it must be made from the rest of the first list plus the second list; that is, it must be made from

```
(2 3)     and     (4 5)
```

Perhaps you can see that the 'somehow' is actually another instance of appending lists!

Exercise

Now try to write the definition of `(X Y) append-to Z`. Write one sentence to cover the case where `X` is empty, and another for when it is non-empty. The second will be a rule which has the consequence `((x1|X1) Y) append-to (x1|Z)` together with a single `append-to` condition which relates `Z` to `X1` and `Y` (see Figure 5.4).

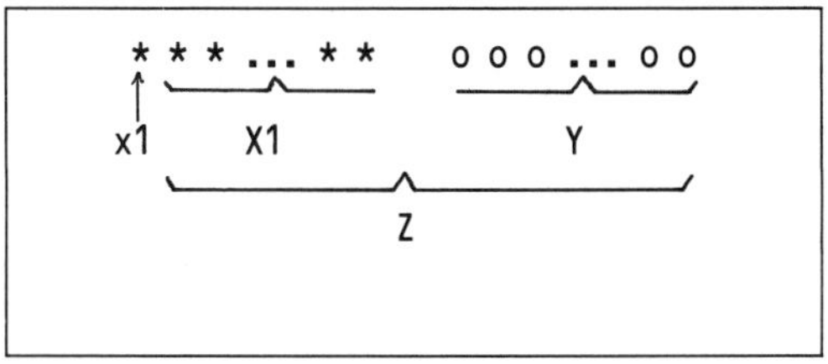

Fig. 5.4

Solution

These two English sentences cover all cases between them:

(a) If the first list is empty, then the result of appending the two lists is just the second list.

(b) If the first list is non-empty, then we can represent it as `(x1|X1)`, say. The result of appending this to a list `Y` is `(x1|Z)`, where `Z` is the result of appending `X1` to `Y`.

The second rule here is made clearer by looking at another example. What the rule is saying is that the result of appending, say,

`(A B C)` and `(D E)`

is a list `(A|Z)`, where `Z` is the list formed by appending `(B C)` to `(D E)`. That is, we glue the first member of the first list on to the list given by appending the tail of the first list to the second list.

Having thought through the logic, the hard part is over. Translating the above into two PROLOG sentences is easy:

```
(() Y) append-to Y                                          (1)
((x1|X1) Y) append-to (x1|Z) if (X1 Y) append-to Z          (2)
```

Now to check that it works. The best way as usual is to type it into a PROLOG computer and try some queries, like these:

```
(a)  which(x : ((fe fi) (fo fum)) append-to x)
     (fe fi fo fum)
     No (more) answers

(b)  is(((A B C) (D E)) append-to (A B C D E))
     YES
```

By experimenting a little, we will see that append-to is invertible to a remarkable degree:

```
(c)  which(x : ((P R) x) append-to (P R O L O G))
     (O L O G)
     No (more) answers

(d)  which(y : (y (ti ta)) append-to (tum tum ti ta))
     (tum tum)
     No (more) answers

(e)  which(x1 x2 : (x1 x2) append-to (C O W))
     () (C O W)
     (C) (O W)
     (C O) (W)
     (C O W) ()
     No (more) answers

(f)  which(x1 x2 : (x1 (I|x2)) append-to (S I L I C O N))
     (S) (L I C O N)
     (S I L) (C O N)
     No (more) answers
```

Study these examples, and check mentally that PROLOG's answers are correct.

All this invertibility makes append-to an extremely powerful program. As the queries show, it can be used for splitting a list as well as for joining two lists together. The flow diagrams in Figure 5.5 illustrate its usages corresponding to the query goals (a)–(e) above. A good idea is to follow a goal evaluation through with SIMTRACE; the essence of how PROLOG gets it to work is that, if the first list is non-empty, then rule 2 will result in an `append-to` goal with **a shorter first list**. Eventually, the first list becomes empty and then sentence 1 gives the second list as an unconditional answer, allowing PROLOG to 'glue on' the successive first terms which have been queuing up.

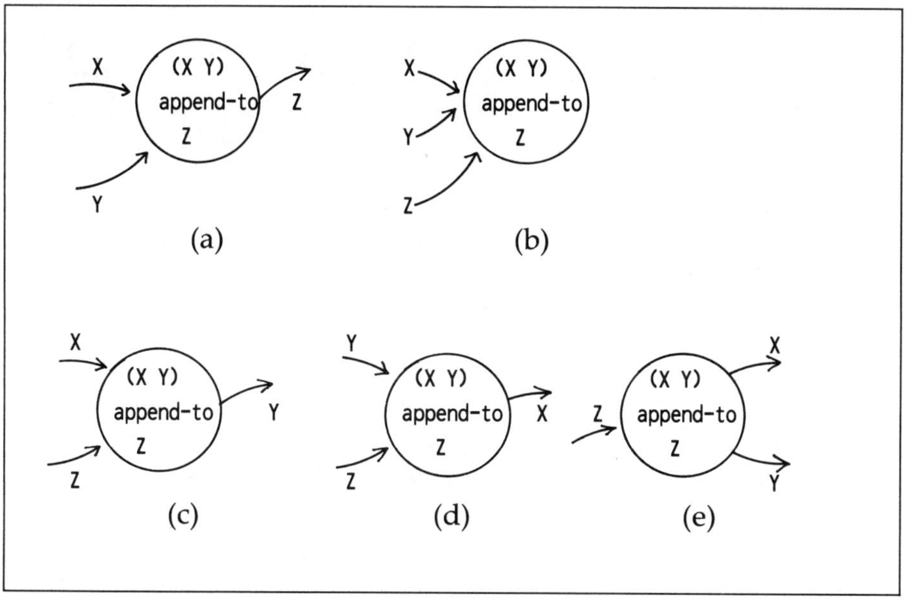

Fig. 5.5

`reverses-to`

The list notation makes it easy to get at the front members of a list, but getting at the back is more difficult. This is where `reverses-to` helps out. An example of a `reverses-to` relationship is

```
(1 2 3 4) reverses-to (4 3 2 1)
```

and in general, `X reverses-to Y` holds when the list `Y` is the reverse of the list `X`.

Studying that example more closely should help us to write a definition. How can the first list be transformed into the second? Look again at that first list: the head is `1` and the tail is `(2 3 4)`. If we reverse the tail we get `(4 3 2)`, which is very close to the second list.

Suppose we 'wrap up' the head into the list `(1)`; we now have two lists:

`(4 3 2)` and `(1)`

The relation between these two lists and the required list `(4 3 2 1)` is one that you may recognize!

Exercise

Write the definition of `X reverses-to Y`, and try your theories out on a computer if at all possible. As a clue, don't forget that not every list can be split: we need a special sentence for the empty list. If the list is non-empty, then we can write it as `(x|X)`, which will reverse to a list `Y` (say) if `X` reverses to some list `X1` and `Y` is the result of appending `X1` to the list which has `x` as its only member.

Solution

Two English sentences are

(a) The empty list is the reverse of itself.

(b) `(x|X)` reverses to `Y` if `X` reverses to `X1` and `X1` and `(x)` append to `Y`.

The purpose of the append is to 'glue' the term `x` on to the back of the list `X1`. Notice that we append `X1` to `(x)`, and not to `x`; the reason is that `append-to` expects its arguments to be lists, and enclosing the term `x` in brackets satisfies this requirement.

Translating into PROLOG gives

```
() reverses-to ()                                        (1)
(x|X) reverses-to Y if                                   (2)
                    X reverses-to X1  &
                    (X1 (x)) append-to Y
```

Before we test our definition, let's try to anticipate whether it will work. The main type of goal we have in mind for the relation is shown in Figure 5.6 — the first list is an input and the second an output. Can we draw a sensible flow diagram for the second rule with this usage? Figure 5.7 shows that we can. The input to the whole program is

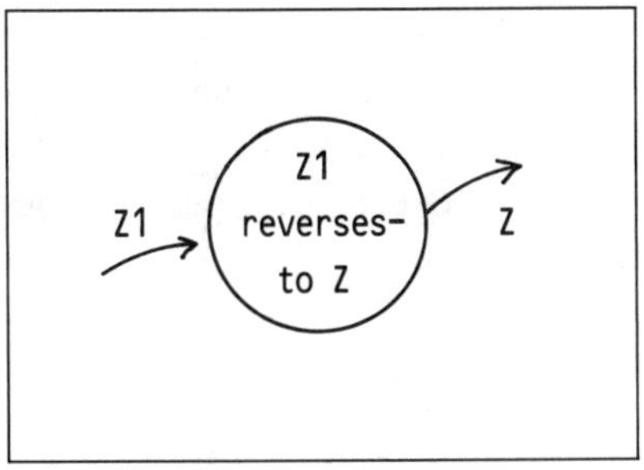

Fig. 5.6

(x|X); the first condition takes X as input and it outputs X1; the second condition takes X1 and x as inputs and it outputs Y; and Y is the output of the main goal. So the flow of replacements is consistent. Notice that the first condition is itself a reverses-to condition, but its input is a **smaller** list than the list which is input to the main goal (it is X as opposed to (x|X)). This is good, because it suggests that eventually the empty list will be input, and then the first reverses-to sentence will provide an output. Notice also that the usage of append-to is one we have just established in the last section, in that two lists are inputs and the joined-up list is output; we know that append-to can deliver the goods in this situation.

Of course, the real test is on the computer itself. Try this:

```
which(Z:  (D I A N E) reverses-to Z)
(E N A I D)
No (more) answers
```

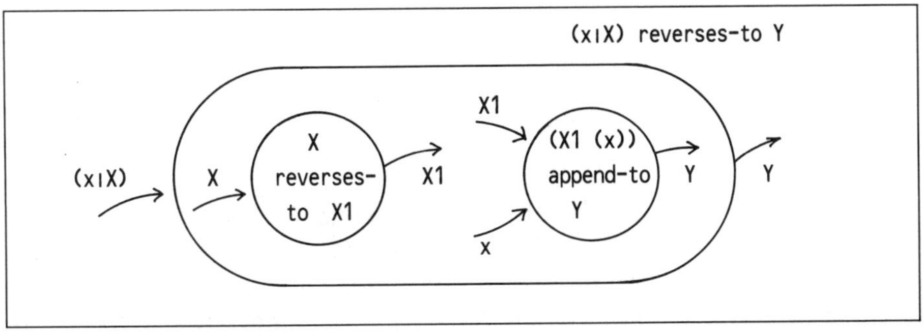

Fig. 5.7

and a few similar queries to see that our program really does work.

Significantly, if the order of the two conditions in the second rule is changed you'll find that the program becomes useless. Draw a flow diagram for this version of the rule and, by looking at the type of `append-to` goal which results, you should see why.

`position-is`

Many other list relations can be defined in terms of the relations which are defined above. As an example, let us consider `position-is`, which relates a member of a list to the position it occupies within the list. For example,

```
(6 (2 4 6 8)) position-is 3
```

is true, and in general `(x X) position-is y` holds when `x` is the `y`th member of the list `X`. A rule in English which defines the relation is

> `x` is in the `y`th position of `X` if `X` can be split into two lists, `X1` and `X2` say, where `X2` begins with `x` and `X1` has y–1 members.

Figure 5.8 is an illustration of this rule.

```
<------------ X --------------->
(..................x..........)
<------- X1 -------><--- X2 --->
        with
         y–1
       members
```

Fig. 5.8

Once we are satisfied that the rule offers a good definition, we begin to translate into PROLOG. The consequence is, of course, `(x X) position-is y`, but the conditions need some thought. On close inspection, we can actually see three. Let us set them down, first in English:

(a) X is split into two lists, X1 and X2.
(b) X2 begins with x.
(c) X1 has y–1 members.

The first condition can be translated into (X1 X2) append-to X (remember how we used append-to earlier to find splittings of the list (C O W), for example). The second we will simply write as X2 begins-with x, where begins-with is a relation which we hope to be able to define later. That lets us move at once to the final condition. At first this one seems tricky, because an expression such as y-1 is not allowed as a PROLOG term; but fortunately we can separate the condition into two parts:

(c1) X1 has y1 (say) members, and
(c2) y1 plus 1 is y.

which are easily translated as X1 length-is y1 and SUM(y1 1 y) respectively.

Now that we have translations of the consequence and the conditions, the PROLOG version of the rule can be set down:

```
(x X) position-is y if
                        (X1 X2) append-to X  &
                        X2 begins-with x  &
                        X1 length-is y1  &
                        SUM(y1 1 y)
```

Finally, how should we define begins-with? Consider: for any list X, the relation X begins-with x will hold if x is equal to the head of X. The tail can be anything — call it Z, say. So

```
X begins-with x if X EQ (x|Z)
```

should do perfectly well, although

```
(x|X) begins-with x
```

is a simpler alternative which has the very same meaning. Either one will do. (We could even replace the first two position-is conditions by the single condition (X1 (x|X2)) append-to X, thereby taking an even bigger short cut.)

The program must now be tested with a few queries. Try, for example,

```
which(x :  (u (a e i o u)) position-is x)
5
No (more) answers
```

and then verify that the program is invertible, with a query like

```
which(x :  (x (9 8 7 6 5)) position-is 3)
7
No (more) answers
```

Finally, let's consider an example in which `position-is` could be useful. Look back for a moment to the FRONT-ROW database on page 51, in which we described the seating places of the group of friends by a set of six facts. An alternative would be to write the single fact

```
(Jill Bob Tony Tracey Ian Mary Sam) is-row
```

in which the sequence of places is represented by a list. Then to define the `left-of` relation we could have used a single rule like this:

```
x left-of y if
             Z is-row  &
             (x Z) position-is x1  &
             (y Z) position-is y1  &
             SUM(x1 1 y1)
```

Try it!

RECURSIVE RELATIONS

Many of the standard list relations treated above are defined partly in terms of themselves. For example, look again at the definition of `length-is`:

```
() length-is 0                                    (1)
(z|Z) length-is y if                              (2)
                   Z length-is y1  &
                   SUM(y1 1 y)
```

One of the conditions of the second rule is itself a `length-is` condition; the definition of the relation refers to the same relation. Definitions which have this property are called **recursive** definitions and relations so defined are known as recursive relations. Recursiveness, or recursion for short, is often a natural feature of the description of relations. Consider for example the logical interpretation of the second `length-is` rule:

> The list `(z|Z)` has `y` members if the list `Z` has `y1` members and `y` is one more than `y1`.

Undoubtedly, this rule corresponds with our intuitive notion of the length of a list: the length is one greater if the list has one extra member. It is an obviously correct description. But whether it makes a good program, in the sense that PROLOG can actually use it to compute the length of a given list, is another matter. To anticipate the answer we must consider the procedural interpretation of the rule, which is

> To solve the goal `(z|Z) length-is y`, solve `Z length-is y1 & SUM(y1 1 y)`.

Figure 5.9 illustrates this procedure when a list `(z|Z)` is the goal input and `y` is an output. To solve the goal `(z|Z) length-is y`, PROLOG immediately tries to solve `Z length-is y1`: notice that this is a goal of the same type, but the goal input is now a list which is shorter by one member. Eventually, this process will result in the empty list, which will give a straight answer by the first rule so that the `SUM` goals which have been queuing up can be tackled. The very last `SUM` goal to be tackled will output the answer to the problem.

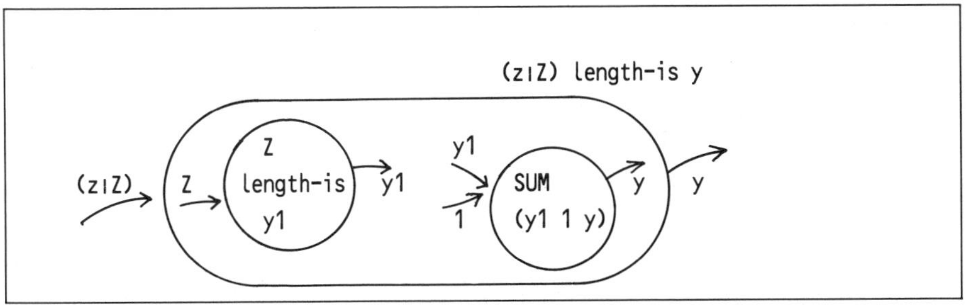

Fig. 5.9

The `length-is` example illustrates two important points about recursive definitions of relations. First, a non-recursive sentence for the relation, one which gives a 'straight answer', is usually essential; without such a sentence, goals will either always fail, or else their evaluation will last forever (or for as long as your computer's memory has queuing space). Second, notice how the recursive second rule above produced new goals with inputs which were getting nearer and nearer to the non-recursive case. This is a very good sign, since it suggests that the evaluation will eventually reach an end.

Exercise

Most people find that it takes a while to become skilled at working with lists. Practice helps. Try now to write PROLOG definitions for each of the following relations. Each one can be defined by one sentence which caters for a special case, together with a recursive general sentence. Figure 5.10 shows the types of goals which your programs should be able to solve: test out your answers on a computer if possible.

(a) `product-is`, where `X product-is y` holds if `X` is a list of numbers which multiply together to give `y`.

(b) `is-uniform`, where `X is-uniform` holds if `X` is a list containing identical numbers or words (such as `(hello hello hello)`).

(c) `is-ordered`, where `X is-ordered` holds if `X` is a list of numbers which are in strictly ascending order.

(d) `max-is`, where `X max-is z` holds if `X` is a list of numbers of which `z` is the maximum.

(e) `adjacent-on`, where `(x y) adjacent-on Z` holds if `x` and `y` are consecutive terms of a list `Z` (for example `(O L) adjacent-on (P R O L O G)` is true).

THE `int-in` RELATION

As another example of a recursive definition, which this time is not a list relation, consider the standard `int-in` relation. `x int-in (y z)` holds when `x` is an integer in the inclusive interval between two integers `y` and `z`. These two English rules together form a description of the relation:

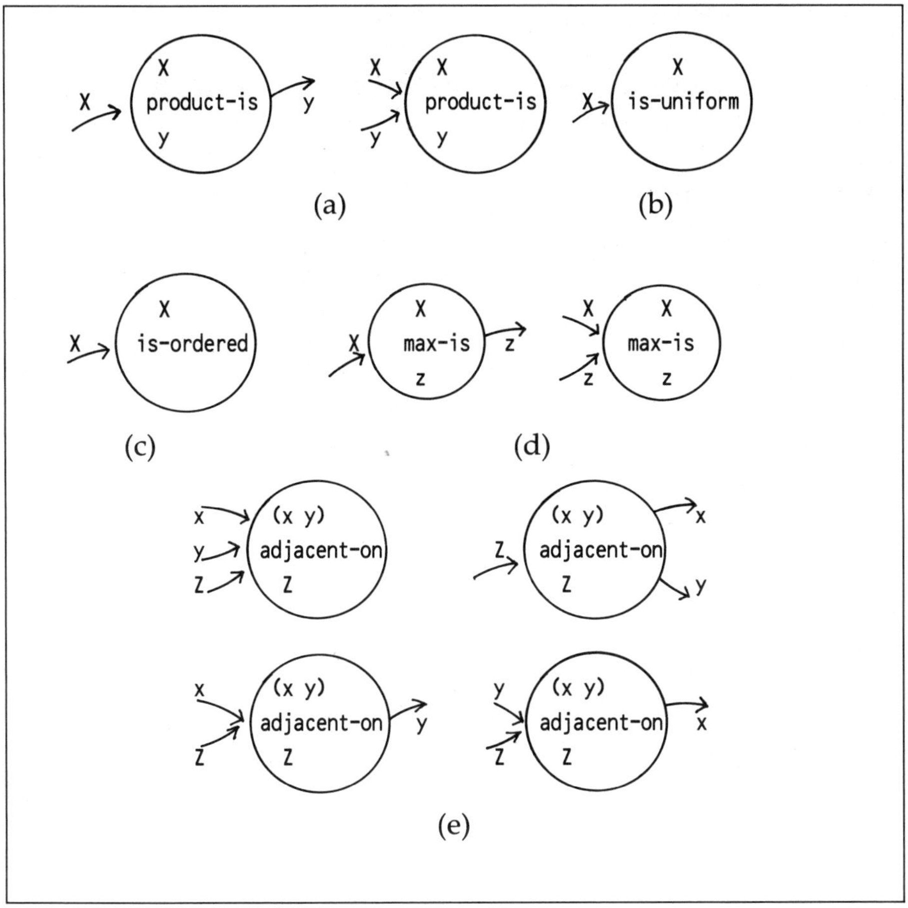

Fig. 5.10

(a) x is an integer in any interval starting with x.

(b) x is an integer in (y z) if y is less than z and x is an integer in (y+1 z).

Translating into PROLOG gives

```
x int-in (x y)                                    (1)
x int-in (y z) if                                 (2)
            y LESS z  &
            SUM(y 1 y1)  &
            x int-in (y1 z)
```

The definition is recursive because the second rule itself uses an `int-in` condition. Now, you would be right to think that a much simpler definition of `int-in` is possible (for example, one which just uses two `lessoreq` conditions). The advantage of the definition given is that it provides a program which PROLOG can use to **generate** integers in a given interval. Try it for yourself with the query

```
which(x : x int-in (5 8))
5
6
7
8
No (more) answers
```

This generating use of `int-in` is shown in Figure 5.11(a). The program also has a checking use (Figure 5.11(b)), and it will prove to be very useful.

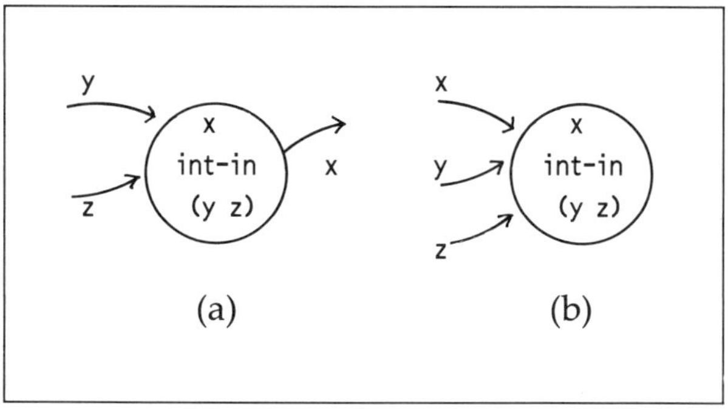

Fig. 5.11

SUMMARY

(1) Lists are terms which can be used to represent complex objects.

(2) Any list except the empty list can be represented by the pattern `(x|X)`, in which `x` is the head of the list (the first member) and `X` is the tail (the list containing all the other members).

(3) Certain list relations, such as `member-of`, `append-to` and `length-is` are so-called standard relations. They are used in many programs.

(4) Relations are often defined recursively — that is, a part of the definition refers to the relation itself.

NOTES

(1) An EQ query will show whether (and how) two lists can be made identical. Try queries such as

```
which(y x : (pies y chips x) EQ (pies eggs chips beans))
```

for example.

(2) 'Program' in this sense means the set of PROLOG sentences (in this case, a set of two rules) which defines a relation.

(3) To be consistent, we should really call the new version a **fact**. But of course, the distinction between a fact and a rule is in a sense artificial: a fact is simply a rule which has zero conditions, as opposed to having one, two, three or whatever.

6 A framework for problem-solving

The previous chapters have equipped us with the fundamentals of PROLOG programming. Now the nuts and bolts part is over. In this chapter we consider how our knowledge and skills might be applied to the activity which PROLOG is all about — the solving of problems.

MAGIC WANDS AND COMMON SENSE

Centuries ago, learned mathematicians and philosophers used to dream of discovering a universal method which would be perfect for solving all problems. Some of them devoted their lives to the search. Needless to say, no such method was ever found. The truth is that there are no magic wands for problem-solving. Instead, problem-solving is a skill which we all have to learn. We begin the learning as soon as we are born, and throughout our lives we get better at it only through our efforts of practise and study.

Someone who has both practiced and studied problem-solving with great success is the mathematician George Polya. Professor Polya, who has written several fine books on the subject (one of which is listed at the back of this book) suggests that the work involved in solving any problem — **any** problem, notice, and not just mathematical problems — can be considered to have four phases. These are shown highlighted in Figure 6.1. Let us consider briefly what characterises each phase.

FOUR PHASES OF PROBLEM-SOLVING
(1) UNDERSTAND THE PROBLEM
(2) DEVISE A PLAN OF THE SOLUTION
(3) CARRY OUT THE PLAN
(4) LOOK BACK AT THE SOLUTION

Fig. 6.1

(1) The first phase is to make sure that you **understand the problem**. Most importantly, you must see what is required of a solution. The point here is that if you don't clearly see what the problem is about to begin with, then your chances of solving it are very slim.

(2) Next, you should study the way in which the various objects in the problem are related. Look for a link between what is known and what is required. This should lead you to **make a plan of the solution**. Without some kind of plan, you will be reduced to looking at details willy-nilly. That way the solution is unlikely to be discovered unless you happen to bump into it by chance.

(3) Now, **carry out** your plan. Check each step to make sure that an error does not prevent you from reaching the solution.

(4) Finally, **look back** upon the solution. Make certain that the result is correct, and consider how the experience of having solved the problem could be of use to you in the future.

Obviously, this scheme has nothing to do with magic. Really it amounts to good common sense. Yet it is surprising how often people overlook common sense in the face of a new problem and take to panic instead.

How can these ideas be applied to the business of problem-solving with PROLOG? They can help by providing a general framework. The easiest way to illustrate this is to work through an example. Later we shall return to discuss the problem-solving framework in a more general way.

EXAMPLE: A MYSTERY NUMBER

Problem: A certain number has two digits. When the number formed by writing the digits backwards is subtracted from it, the answer is 72. Find the number.

Understanding the problem

What is required in this problem is to find an unknown object, a certain number. Let us clarify the problem with an example: 43 is as good a two-digit number as any. Reversing its digits gives 34. Now 43 minus 34 is not 72, so 43 is not the number we are looking for — and nor did we expect to be so lucky as to strike on the answer with the guess; the point was to help us to understand the problem.

Let us set down the conditions which a number would need to satisfy, in order to be the required number.

(1) It must have two digits.

(2) When the number is written backwards, the result is a number 72 less than the original.

We seem now to understand the problem well enough. It's time to start thinking about a plan.

Devising a plan

Let x represent the unknown number. Then we could express the problem in PROLOG as

```
x is-answer
```

say; this being a goal which we wish to solve for x (see Figure 6.2).

Eventually, we will want to be able to query

```
which(x :  x is-answer)
```

and have the answer pop up on the screen. To make this possible, we must write a sentence for `is-answer` which describes `x` in terms of the conditions which we set down above. So the next step is to translate these conditions into PROLOG.

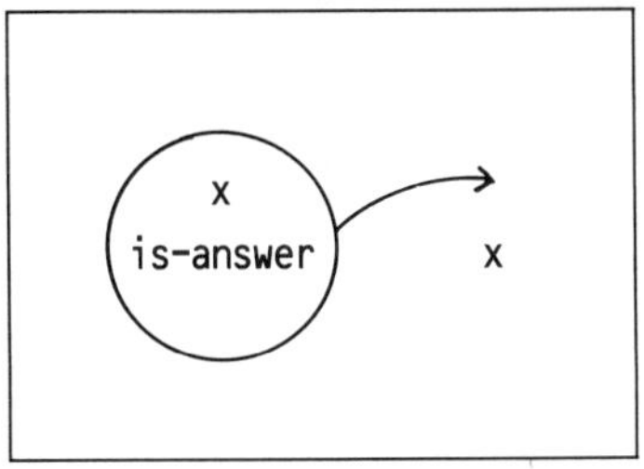

Fig. 6.2

(1) For the first condition, `x has-two-digits` is as good a translation as any.

(2) The second condition is really two conditions. Letting `y` represent the 'backwards' number, we can translate the first of these as `x backwards-is y` and the second as `72 difference-of (x y)`, say.

That gives us the PROLOG description

```
x is-answer if
              x has-two-digits  &
              x backwards-is y  &
              72 difference-of (x y)
```

But will it work? Will PROLOG be able to use this rule to find a replacement for `x`? The flow diagram in Figure 6.3 shows how it could. We will need to provide definitions for these relations:

(1) `has-two-digits`, the program for which must be capable of generating all two-digit numbers.

(2) `backwards-is`, which must output the reverse of a given number.

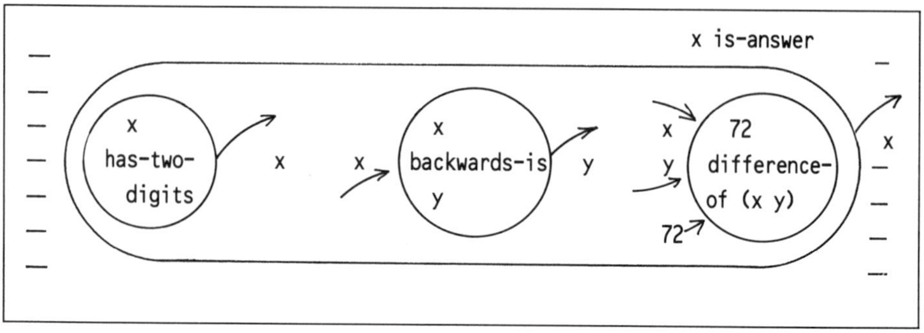

Fig. 6.3

(3) `difference-of`, which must be able to check whether two given numbers have a difference of 72.

At this point, we begin to feel much more confident of eventually solving the problem. The reason is that **we have a plan**. The plan is to write the required definitions, type them into our computer and enter the above mentioned query. Providing we carry out the plan with sufficient care, making sure to check each step, there is no reason why it should not succeed.

Carrying out the plan

Let us consider one at a time the relations we need to define.

(1) `has-two-digits`

A description of this relation, expressed in English, is

A number has two digits if it lies inclusively between 10 and 99.

Does that suggest a familiar relation? On page 94 we discussed `int-in`, the standard integer relation. It will help us here. We can translate the above into PROLOG as

```
x has-two-digits if x int-in (10 99)
```

which certainly looks correct. But will it work? As you can see from Figure 6.3, our plan requires that the `has-two-digits` program should be able to generate two-digit numbers. Figure 6.4 shows how the above rule will make this possible. It relies on the known ability of `int-in` to output integers in a given interval. As a further check, we can type the sentence above into a computer, along with the standard `int-in` definition, and try the query

```
which(x : x has-two-digits)
```

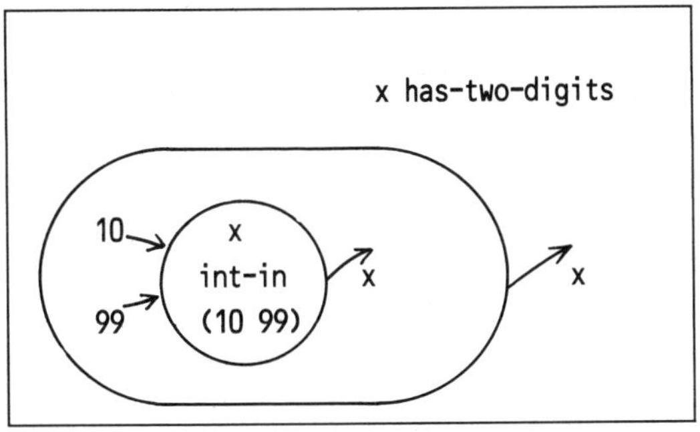

Fig. 6.4

(2) `backwards-is`

Before defining `x backwards-is y`, first consider that a two-digit number has a tens digit and a units digit. We might say, for example, that 4 tens with 2 units `compose` the number 42, and that 50 `decomposes` to 5 tens with 0 units. Introducing these two relations makes it easier to write (in English) a description of the `backwards-is` relation:

> An integer `x` backwards is `y` if `x` decomposes to `z1` tens with `z2` units, say, and `z2` tens with `z1` units compose the integer `y`.

Now, translating into PROLOG:

```
x backwards-is y if
                   x decomposes-to (z1 z2)  &
                   (z2 z1) compose y
```

which looks correct. But will it work? According to our plan, the `backwards-is` program must output a replacement for its second argument when supplied with a number for its first. Now, Figure 6.5 shows how this type of goal could be solved using the rule above. We will need to define two further relations, as shown by

(1) `x decomposes-to (y z)`, which can output a list pair of integers `(y z)` given an integer `x`;

(2) `(x y) compose z`, which can output `z` given `(x y)`.

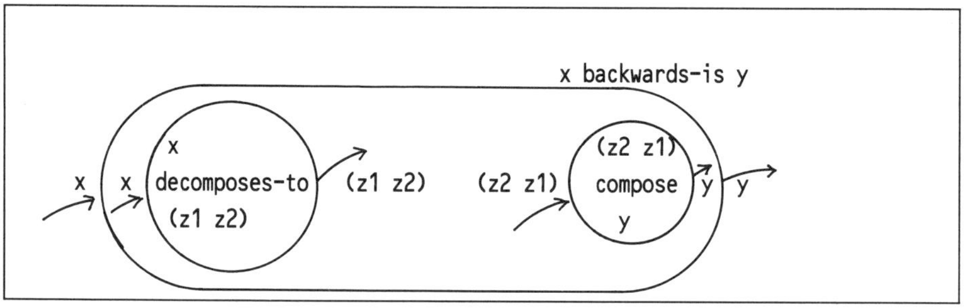

Fig. 6.5

Since these two are really inverse relations (in that each one 'undoes' the other), we might have tried to combine them in a single predicate with an invertible program. But that could be quite tricky, since the arithmetic relations, with their known restrictions, would certainly be involved. Our approach looks to be a safer bet.

We now have a **sub-plan**. We have two further relations to define, the programs for which must be able to solve goals of the type shown in Figure 6.5. Let us now carry out this sub-plan.

(2.1) `decomposes-to`

An English description of the relation is

> An integer `x` decomposes to `(y z)` if `x` has a tens digit of `y` and a units digit of `z`.

We can translate this into PROLOG as

```
x decomposes-to (y z) if
                        x has-tens-digit y  &
                        x has-units-digit z
```

Remember that our plan requires `decomposes-to` to be able to output the decomposition when the integer is supplied. Will the rule we have written work? The flow diagram in Figure 6.6 shows that, providing we can write definitions for

(1) `has-tens-digit`, which can output the tens digit of a given integer; and

(2) `has-units-digit`, which can do the same for the units digit,

then it should work perfectly well. So now we have a **sub-sub-plan** to carry out!

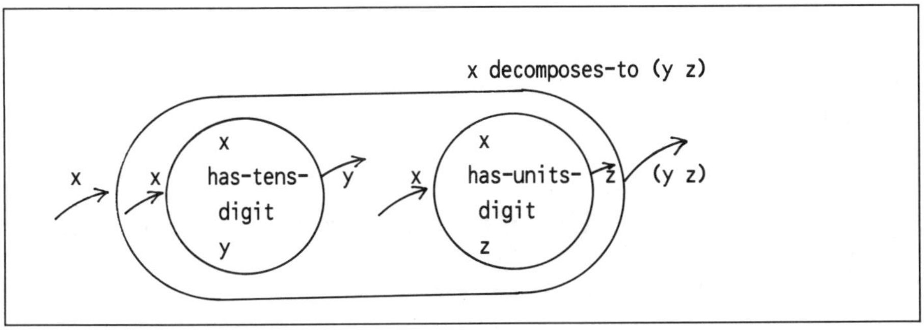

Fig. 6.6

(2.1.1) `has-tens-digit`

An English description of the relation is

> An integer `x` has a tens digit `y` if 10 divided into `x` is `z`, say, and the integer part of `z` is `y`.

In PROLOG, we write the conditions using the built-in relations `SUM` and `INT`:

```
x has-tens-digit y if
                    TIMES(z 10 x)  &
                    z INT y
```

This is a step which we can check immediately with a query. Type in the definition of `has-tens-digit`, and try

```
which(x : 73 has-tens-digit x)
```

to make sure that the program can solve goals of the type required by our plan.

(2.1.2) `has-units-digit`

An example of the relationship is

```
68 has-units-digit 8
```

Again, we begin by describing the relation in English. We might try

> `x` has a units digit `y` if `x` has a tens digit `z`, say, and if 10 times `z` is `y` less than `x`.

The condition after the 'and' here looks tricky. Let us introduce another variable to represent '10 times `z`', so as to spell out precisely what it means:

> `x` has a units digit `y` if `x` has a tens digit `z`, say, and if 10 times `z` is `y1`, say, and `y1` is `y` less than `x`.

Now we feel happier about a PROLOG translation:

```
x has-units-digit y if
                    x has-tens-digit z  &
                    TIMES(10 z y1)  &
                    SUM(y1 y x)
```

Now, does it work as required by the plan? A few queries, using `has-units-digit` goals of the type shown in Figure 6.6, such as

```
which(x : 30 has-units-digit x)
```

will show that it does.

We have now completed the `decomposes-to` part of the plan. As Figure 6.5 reminds us, the program will be expected to output the two digits of a given integer. Therefore, we should test it with a query such as

```
which(y z :  27 decomposes-to (y z))
```

to make sure that all is well.

(2.2) `compose`

An example of a `compose` relationship is `(2 4) compose 24`. Let us set down an English description of the relation:

> The digits `(x y)` compose the integer 10x + `y`.

This description is logically sound, but it cannot be immediately translated into PROLOG since the expression `10x + y` is not an allowed term. However, with a little re-statement the sentence becomes

> The digits `(x y)` compose the integer `z` if 10 times `x` is `x1`, say, and `x1` plus `y` is `z`.

Notice again how the introduction of extra variables helps. The translation now is easy:

```
(x y) compose z if
                   TIMES(10 x x1)  &
                   SUM(x1 y z)
```

Looking at Figure 6.5, we see that the `compose` program is required to output `z` when `x` and `y` are inputs. So let us query, say

```
which(x :  (3 4) compose x)
```

to check that it works.

We have now completed the `backwards-is` sub-plan. Test it out with a query such as

```
which(x :  29 backwards-is x)
```

and a few others like it. These tests will show that `backwards-is` can be used as required by our plan.

(3) `difference-of`

The obvious way to define this relation is to express it in terms of **SUM**, like this:

```
z difference-of (x y) if SUM(y z x)
```

Figure 6.3 reminds us that our plan only requires a program which can solve `difference-of` goals in which all the arguments are inputs. Hence, the restrictions on **SUM** won't affect us here. A query such as

```
is(23 difference-of (45 22))
```

will confirm that the definition above is adequate.

And that finishes the job. All the loose ends have been tied up. We have carried the plan through to the end, and all that remains now is for us to enter

```
which(x :  x is-answer)
```

and let the computer do the rest!

Looking back at the solution

For convenience, Figure 6.7 shows the completed program.(1) We can judge it to be a good program on two points. First, it is a logically correct description. Second, it is a description which PROLOG can use successfully to solve the problem. Logical considerations came first in the development of the program, but notice that we never forgot to check that PROLOG would be able to **use** our descriptions.

Let us look briefly back at the exercise and see what we have learned.

(a) First, have you checked that the answers are correct?

(b) How useful is the result? In itself, we have to admit that it is unlikely to be of much use. The discovery of a number which is 72 more than its own reverse is not a very significant mathematical discovery.

(c) How valuable are the relations which we have defined in solving the problem? They could perhaps be helpful in some future problems. Certainly, we should keep a careful record of each problem we tackle. To build up a library of programs for relations, each with flow diagrams to show the types of goal which

```
x is-answer if
            x has-two-digits  &
            x backwards-is y  &
            72 difference-of (x y)

x has-two-digits if x int-in (10 99)

x backwards-is y if
            x decomposes-to (z1 z2)  &
            (z2 z1) compose y

x decomposes-to (y z) if
            x has-tens-digit y  &
            x has-units-digit z

x has-tens-digit y if
            TIMES(z 10 x)  &
            z INT y

x has-units-digit y if
            x has-tens-digit z  &
            TIMES(z 10 y1)  &
            SUM(y1 y x)

(x y) compose z if
            TIMES(x 10 x1)  &
            SUM(x1 y z)

z difference-of (x y) if SUM(y z x)
```

Fig. 6.7 The completed program.

can be solved, is very worthwhile. But notice that with an eye to the future, we would have done better to consider more general versions of the relations in the problem. For example, if instead of `x has-two-digits` we had written a definition for `x has-digits y`, where `y` would be replaced by 2 here but could actually be any positive integer, then this would be a program which might well come in handy later on. A generalization like this one would have involved extra work now, but there is a good chance that it would be well rewarded in the future.

(d) Can the solution be obtained in another way? Yes, the problem can be solved in a few minutes with paper-and-pencil (try it!). Our reason for devoting so much time to it was **to illustrate the methods** of problem-solving with PROLOG. The rest of this chapter considers these methods in a more general context.

THREE TYPES OF PROBLEM

Before going any further, it is helpful to identify three different categories of problem. We shall refer to these categories as **problems-to-find**, **problems-to-prove** and **problems-to-do**.

(a) **Problems-to-find** are those problems which require us to find some unknown object. This object could be a certain number, say, or some particular arrangement of dominoes, or the position of a robot at a given time. The problem tackled in the last section is an example of this category. Usually, **problems-to-find** will correspond to PROLOG goals such as

```
x is-answer
Z is-required-arrangement
Y is-position-at-time 10
```

in which replacements must be found for `x`, `Z` and `Y`.

(b) **Problems-to-prove** are problems which require us to prove the truth of some relationship or **conjecture**. For example, we may have to show that a given triangle is a right-angled triangle, or that a particular route between two towns on a map is the shortest route, or that a given date is a valid date. PROLOG goals such as

```
(5 12 13) is-right-angled
(London Dover Paris) is-shortest-route-between (London Paris)
(30 2 1985) is-invalid-date
```

are typical goals corresponding to **problems-to-prove**. These goals should succeed only if the corresponding conjecture can be proved.

(c) **Problems-to-do** are those in which the requirement is for the computer to carry out some procedure or other — for instance, the computer is to draw a house on the screen, or to print out a calendar for a given year, or to play a game of chess against a human opponent. The PROLOG goals corresponding to these problems might be

```
house is-drawn
1986 calendar-is-printed
chess is-played
```

The goal in a **problem-to-do** is not really a 'relationship': it is the name of a procedure which is described by a matching rule. The tail of the rule gives the sequence of steps which make up the procedure. Because **problems-to-do** are mainly concerned with controlling the computer's behaviour (and not with the truth or falsehood of relationships) we call them **non-logical** problems.

A GENERAL FRAMEWORK

As we said earlier, there is no magic wand for solving problems. However, the problem which we tackled earlier showed that the four-phase scheme of Professor Polya suggests a general framework for problem-solving with PROLOG. It doesn't answer all our questions, but it does at least suggest some useful questions to ask. In this section we look at this framework in more detail.

Understand the problem

Forget PROLOG at this stage: all your earliest thinking about a problem should be in English.

You should know what **type** of problem is the one to be solved, and you should be clear about what is required.

> If it is a **problem-to-find**, what is the unknown? What conditions must the unknown satisfy? Can you separate the conditions and write down each one?
>
> If it is a **problem-to-prove**, what conjecture is required to be proved? Can you write down some conditions which, if they were each proved, would together prove the conjecture?
>
> If it is a **problem-to-do**, what is the required procedure? Can you write down a sequence of steps which together would make up the procedure?

Only when you are satisfied that you can answer these questions should you start thinking about a plan to solve the problem.

Devise a plan

(a) The first stage in devising a plan is to find a suitable PROLOG way in which to **represent the objects** which occur in the problem.

An unknown object will be represented by a variable. Simple objects will correspond to numbers or words: complex objects will correspond to some kind of list.

(b) Ask yourself: **What is the goal?**

(i) Decide upon a PROLOG goal which seems to correspond to your problem. Make the goal as general as necessary — that is, it should represent the **type** of goal which will actually be solved.

(ii) Draw a flow diagram to show which of the goal's arguments will actually be inputs and which will be outputs.

(iii) Write down the query (or an example of the type of query) which you are working towards — the query with which you hope eventually to obtain the solution to your problem.

(c) Now, in PROLOG, **write a description of the relationship** represented by the goal. Usually, this takes the form of a single rule with the goal at the head; the tail should be a straightforward translation of the conditions or steps which you identified earlier. More specifically

(i) In a **problem-to-find**, the tail will contain PROLOG translations of the conditions for the unknown, so that a rule such as

```
x is-answer if
            x has-two-digits  &
            x backwards-is y  &
            72 difference-of (x y)
```

(to take the example of page 100) will be obtained.

(ii) In a **problem-to-prove**, the tail will contain PROLOG translations of the conditions which together prove the conjecture; so a rule something like

```
(x y z) is-right-angled if
                      x squared-is x1  &
                      y squared-is y1  &
                      z squared-is z1  &
                      SUM(x1 y1 z1)
```

might result.

(iii) In a **problem-to-do**, the tail will comprise PROLOG translations of the steps which make up the required procedure; a rule such as

```
house is-drawn if
              wall is-drawn  &
              roof is-drawn  &
              chimney is-drawn
```

will be obtained.

(d) Next, ask yourself: **Will it work**? Think about the procedural interpretation of what you have written. Will PROLOG be able to use it to solve your goal? Draw a flow diagram to show how your goal could be solved with your description. Such a flow diagram will also make clear the types of goal which will have to be solved by the programs for the relations which your description has introduced.

You cannot reasonably **guarantee** that your program will work. For one reason, your computer may not have enough memory to complete the evaluation of the goal. But in most cases, you should feel confident about the outcome.

(e) The plan is almost ready. As a last step, make sure that you understand exactly **what is to be done**. Ask yourself again

> What relations need to be defined?
> What types of goal must the programs for these relations be able to solve?
> What query are you working towards?

Carry out the plan

You must provide a suitable PROLOG definition for each needed relation. For each relation,

(a) Write a precise English description of the relation. (It may help to write one or two rough versions first.)

(b) Translate the precise English description into PROLOG sentences. You now have a program for the relation.

(c) Refer to your plan to see what type of goal this program will be expected to solve. Look at the program you have written and ask yourself: Will it work? It often helps to draw a flow diagram to show how solutions will be obtained.

(d) Does your definition require that further relations be defined? If so, you now have a **sub-plan** to carry out.

(e) Enter the PROLOG definition into your computer. Check that it works with a few queries for goals of the appropriate type.

Before trying to define a relation, it often helps to play around with a few examples of it. Ask yourself questions like these:

(1) Have you seen the relation before? Have you seen a similar relation?

(2) Can you separate the definition into two or more cases for the relation? If so, can you write a sentence to describe each case?

(3) Can you describe a special case of the relation — perhaps when a list is empty, or a number is zero? If so, can you also write down a general case — possibly one in which the relation is defined in terms of itself (that is, recursively)?

(4) Can you make use of the standard relations? Can you use the built-in relations? Can you use any relation you have defined before?

When writing rules, a rough guide is that the number of conditions should be two, three or four. If you write a rule with only one condition, ask yourself: What new, useful idea is being introduced? If you write a rule with more than four conditions, ask yourself: Could a simpler rule be written, one which leaves the analysis of some of the detail until later?

Look back at the solution

The experience of solving a problem should add to your abilities as a problem-solver. To get the most benefit from the experience, take a critical look back at the work you have completed. Ask yourself

(a) Is the solution correct? Has it been checked?

(b) How useful is the result?

(c) How useful are the relations you have defined? Are they likely to be valuable in the future? Have you generalised them sufficiently?

(d) How powerful (that is, invertible) is your program for each relation? Would it have been possible to write a more powerful version?

(e) Is there another way to solve the problem with PROLOG? How would it have been solved without a computer?

TOP-DOWN DESCRIPTION

A PROLOG program is a description of a problem to be solved. The problem-solving framework which is outlined above involves the development of description **downwards**, starting from the broadest expression of the whole problem and ending with the definition of small detail. A descriptive process of this kind is known as a **top-down description**.

To illustrate, consider again the problem tackled on page100. The tree diagram in Figure 6.8 shows how the various relations which appeared in the description of the problem were introduced. First of all came `is-answer`, which we defined in terms of the relations `has-two-digits`, `backwards-is` and `difference-of`. We call `is-answer` the `top-level` relation: writing its definition provided the broad description of the whole problem from which everything else followed. Next, `has-two-digits` was defined in terms of `int-in`. Since `int-in` is a standard relation, no more work was necessary on that branch of the tree. Then, `backwards-is` was defined in terms of `decomposes-to` and `compose`; then `decomposes-to` was defined in terms of `has-tens-digit` and `has-units-digit`; and so on. You can see that at the tip of each branch of the tree sits either a built-in relation, or a standard relation, or a relation which has already been defined: when we reach these points we know that no further description on that branch is required.

Notice that our strategy followed each branch all the way down to the tips before developing another branch. For instance, we pursued the `backwards-is` branch to the finish before starting on `difference-of`. This is known as **depth-first** top-down description.[2] An alternative form of top-down description, called **breadth-first**, develops all the branches to the same level before going deeper down any one branch: both alternatives have points in their favor.

There is also an alternative to top-down description. We could describe details first and try to assemble larger descriptions by fitting the details together. This way, the tree in Figure 6.8 would be 'grown' starting from below. This is known as **bottom-up** description. Both styles are feasible (and not just in PROLOG, but in English descriptions too) although experience has shown that the top-down approach is usually preferable for problem-solving with PROLOG.

Top-down description is a process of divide-and-conquer. It is mainly concerned with analyzing the logical meanings of relationships and with teasing them apart into collections of less complex relationships. After each stage of description, we have to recall the goals involved and (bearing in mind PROLOG's limitations) ask ourselves: Will it work? Most descriptions will introduce new relations, for which definitions do not yet exist. We have to be confident that when the time comes we will in fact be able to write a good program for each relation. Occasionally one of these will turn out to be a stumbling-block, and then we may be forced to back-track. But we can be certain that, stumbling-blocks apart, the process is relentlessly problem-solving. Eventually all the relationships will have been teased apart into relationships which are trivial to define, because they correspond to facts, built-in relations or whatever. At that point we will recognize that the program is complete and success is reasonably well assured.

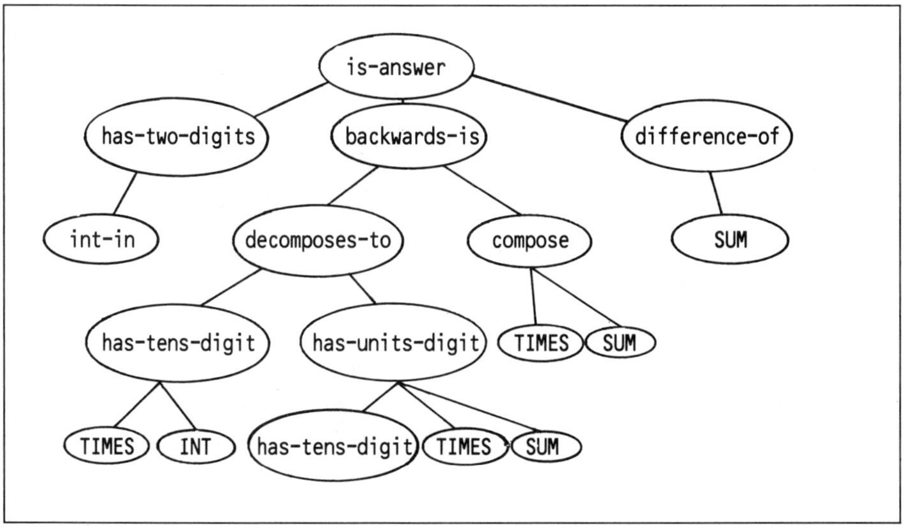

Fig. 6.8 Top-down description tree diagram.

SUMMARY

This chapter has covered a lot of ground, the main points of which are summarized in the following table.

Solving a problem with PROLOG	
PHASE	QUESTIONS TO THINK ABOUT
Understanding the problem	What type of problem is it? What is required? What conditions must be satisfied, or steps carried out?
Devising a plan	How can the objects in the problem be represented? What is the goal? Can you write a description of the relationship represented by the goal? Will it work? What is to be done?
Carrying out the plan	For each needed relation, What is a description of the relation, in English? What is a PROLOG translation of the description? Will it work as required by the plan?
Looking back at the solution	Is the result correct? How useful is the solution? How useful is the program for each relation?

NOTES

(1) To avoid repetition, the definition of the standard relation `int-in` is not included. From here onwards, definitions which appeared earlier in the text will be omitted from program listings.

(2) As the name indicates, there is a close parallel here with PROLOG's depth-first evaluation strategy for goal statements. But to take up that issue would be to digress too far.

7 Some problems solved

The best ways to learn about problem-solving are to study good examples provided by others and to practice solving problems for yourself. This chapter tries to help. It begins with a variety of problems which are solved using the framework described in the last chapter: these are best studied in the sequence in which they appear, although that isn't strictly necessary. It will help for you to follow the problems through with a computer if possible. The chapter ends by suggesting some problems which you might like to try for yourself.

A MAIL-ORDER DATABASE

Problem Sunny Deal Limited have bought a new PROLOG computer system to help with their mail-order business. Their database contains two kinds of sentence. To describe each customer's order, there are facts such as

```
A-R-Tomkins order-is (flange nut wiglet splice)
```

To describe the price of each item, there are facts like

```
flange price-is 2.73
```

Write a program which will find out the amount owed by each customer.

Understanding the problem

This is a **problem-to-find**; what is required is the sum of money owed by any given individual. For example, if the prices of a flange, a nut, a wiglet and a splice are $2.73, $0.10, $0.85 and $2.15 respectively, then the customer `A-R-Tomkins` mentioned above owes

$$\$2.73 + \$0.10 + \$0.85 + \$2.15 = \$5.83$$

altogether.

It seems to be plain enough, but let us make certain that we can write it down in parts. An individual will owe a certain sum of money if

(1) The individual has ordered a particular list of goods, and
(2) The total cost of these goods is the required sum.

Devising a plan

Let `x` represent the name of the individual, and let `y` be the sum of money which he/she is due to pay. Then we could write the goal as

```
x owes y
```

in which `x` will be given and `y` must be found, as shown in the flow diagram in Figure 7.1. Letting `z` denote the list of goods

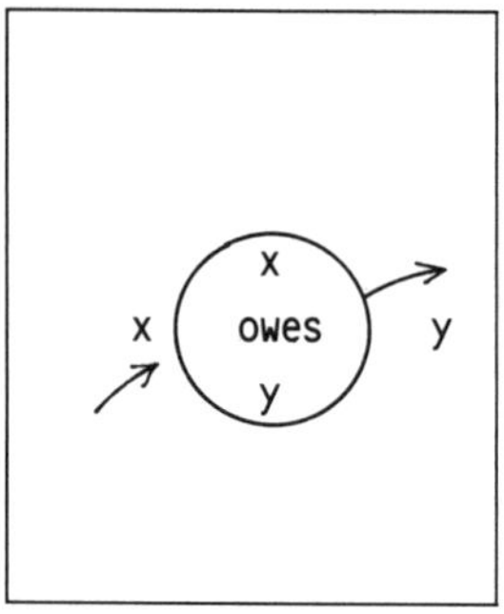

Fig. 7.1

ordered by the customer, we can translate the conditions set out above into PROLOG as

(1) `x order-is z`
(2) `z total-cost-is y`

respectively. Hence, we can write the rule

```
x owes y if
            x order-is z  &
            z total-cost-is y
```

The logic seems to be correct, but will it work? Figure 7.2 shows how it could. The `order-is` facts in the database will supply a list `z` of goods corresponding to a given customer `x`, and all we need do is define a `total-cost-is` relation which can output the amount due for this list. With this plan, Sunny Deal should be able to enter queries like

```
which(x :  A-R-Tomkins owes x)
```

and get back the required information.

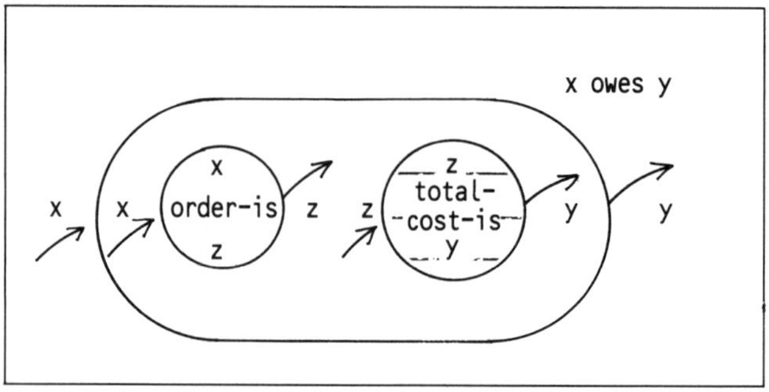

Fig. 7.2

Carrying out the plan

(1) `total-cost-is`

An example of the relationship is

```
(flange nut wiglet splice) total-cost-is 5.83
```

Have we seen a similar relation before? On page 83, we met the `total-is` relation used for summing a list of numbers. We need only modify its definition slightly to get a suitable description of `total-cost-is`. An English description is

(a) The empty list of items has a total cost of zero.

(b) The list `(x|Y)` has a total cost of `z` if the list `Y` has a total cost of `z1`, say, and `z1` plus the price of the item `x` is `z`.

The second of these rules looks a little tricky: let us spell it out further before attempting a PROLOG translation:

(b) The list `(x|Y)` has a total cost of `z` if the list `Y` has a total cost of `z1`, say, and the price of the item `x` is `z2`, say, and `z1` plus `z2` is `z`.

Now the PROLOG definition is easy:

```
() total-cost-is 0
(x|Y) total-cost-is z if
                        Y total-cost-is z1  &
                        x price-is z2  &
                        SUM(z1 z2 z)
```

Will it work? Will PROLOG be able to use this definition as required by our plan (see Figure 7.2) to output the cost of a given list of goods? Looking at the second rule, we see that `total-cost-is` is defined using a `total-cost-is` condition for a **shorter** list (`Y` is one member shorter than `(x|Y)`). This is encouraging, because it suggests that when the rule is used as a procedure the list will eventually become empty, and then the first rule will give a straight answer. A query such as

```
which(x : (flange nut wiglet splice) total-cost-is x)
```

will confirm that the program works when it is added to the database.
That completes the plan. With the sentences shown in Figure 7.3 added to Sunny Deal's database, a query such as

```
which(x : A-R-Tomkins owes x)
```

will produce the required answer.

```
x owes y if
          x order-is z  &
          z total-cost-is y

() total-cost-is 0
(x|Y) total-cost-is z if
          Y total-cost-is z1  &
          x price-is z2  &
          SUM(z1 z2 z)

A-R-Tomkins order-is (flange nut wiglet splice)
...

flange price-is 2.73
nut price-is 0.10
wiglet price-is 0.85
splice price-is 2.15
...
```

Fig. 7.3 The completed program.

Looking back at the solution

(1) A quick check using a calculator should show that PROLOG's answers are correct.

(2) The problem may not have been very interesting, but clearly for Sunny Deal Limited it is a very important problem. Routine database work of this kind is the bread-and-butter of computing

in the commercial world of data processing.

(3) Our program is actually more powerful than was strictly necessary. Sunny Deal can query

```
which(Send x a bill for y :  x owes y)
```

and bills will be generated for all the customers. (Can you modify Figure 7.2 to depict this usage?).

THE RABBIT COLONY

Problem A colony of rabbits lives in Briar's Wood. Their numbers are expected to increase steadily at the rate of 15% each year. If there are 500 rabbits in 1985, how many are predicted to live in the wood in the year 2000?

Understanding the problem

The problem is a **problem-to-find**. The unknown is the size of the colony in the year 2000; we are given the corresponding number for the year 1985, and told that the growth rate is 15% each year. Let us experiment. In 1986 the population will be

$$500 + 0.15\times500 = 500 + 75 = 575$$

and in 1987 it will be

$$575 + 0.15\times575 = 575 + 86 = 661$$

(this is rounding to the nearest rabbit!). Clearly, by carrying on like this the answer for the year 2000 would emerge eventually, although to work by hand would be very tedious.

It's worth setting down the rules which define the size of the rabbit colony as clearly as we can. The rules are

(1) In 1985, the size is 500.

(2) In any year after 1985, the size is 15% more than the size of the previous year.

Devising a plan

Let y represent the size of the colony in the year x. Then we can write the goal of the problem as

```
x size-is y
```

which must be solved for y when x is given (see Figure 7.4). The problem asks about the year 2000 in particular, but there is no harm in generalizing to cover any year after 1985.

The description which we set out above gives us two rules for the `size-is` relation. The first sets out the special case, which we can write in PROLOG as the fact

```
1985 size-is 500
```

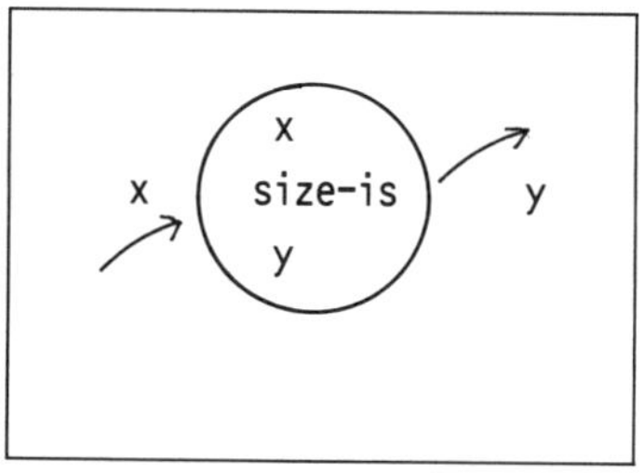

Fig. 7.4

The second is the general rule. A PROLOG translation of it which seems reasonable is

```
x size-is y if
            x after 1985 &
            z year-previous-to x &
            z size-is y1 &
            y fifteen-percent-more-than y1
```

Will PROLOG be able to use these rules to solve our type of goal? Looking at the second rule, it seems that the population for the year 2000 will be computed only when PROLOG can find the population for the year 1999. This in turn depends on PROLOG finding the population for the year 1998, which depends on 1997, and so on.

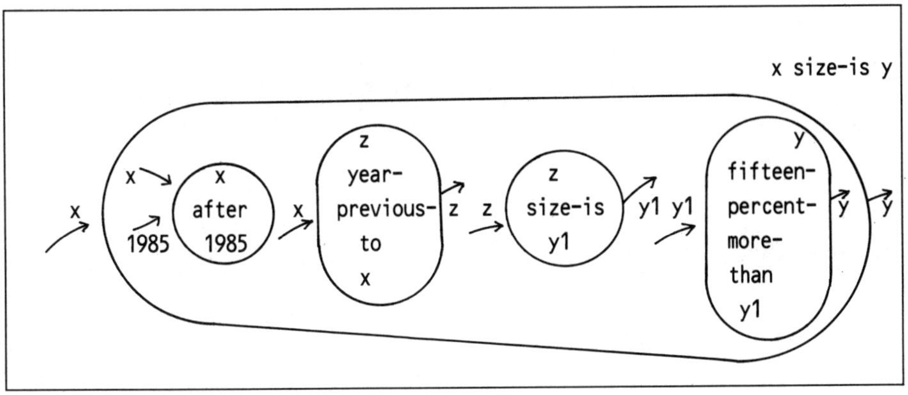

Fig. 7.5

Ultimately all of these depend on PROLOG finding the population for 1985 — but fortunately the first `size-is` sentence will answer that one. This looks promising.

Figure 7.5 shows a flow diagram for the general rule. The `after` relation must be defined so as to check that a given year is after 1985; `year-previous-to` must output the year previous to a given year and `fifteen-percent-more-than` must find a number which is 15% above a given number. With this plan, we should eventually be able to query

```
which(x:  2000 size-is x)
```

and get back the required number of rabbits.

Carrying out the plan

(1) `after`

The obvious English description of the `after` relation is

x is a year after 1985 if 1985 is numerically less than x.

In PROLOG, this becomes

```
x after 1985 if 1985 LESS x
```

Our plan only needs a checking use of `after`, so this definition should be perfectly adequate. A few queries, such as

```
is(1982 after 1985)
```

should show that it works.

(2) `year-previous-to`

An example of this relationship is `1993 year-previous-to 1994`. In English, we can write

> x is the year previous to y if the sum of x and one is y.

A PROLOG translation is

```
x year-previous-to y if SUM(x 1 y)
```

From Figure 7.5 you can see that this rule is required to solve goals in which the second argument of `year-previous-to` is an input. Therefore the `SUM` condition will have two inputs, which will enable it to output a replacement for `x`. Try out the definition with a query like

```
which(x :  x year-previous-to 2000)
```

(3) `fifteen-percent-more-than`

An English description of the relation is

> x is fifteen percent more than y if fifteen percent of y is z, say, and y plus z is x.

The first condition can be easily translated into `TIMES(0.15 y z)`. Then, the PROLOG version of the rule is

```
x fifteen-percent-more-than y if
                         TIMES(0.15 y z)  &
                         SUM(y z x)
```

Figure 7.6 shows how PROLOG should be able to use this rule as required by our plan. A query such as

```
which(x :  x fifteen-percent-more-than 1000)
```

will confirm that it works satisfactorily.

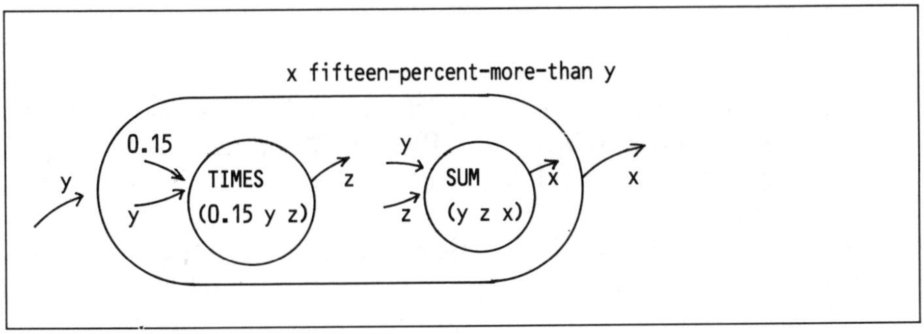

Fig. 7.6

And that finishes the job. Figure 7.7 shows the complete program; all that remains is to query

```
which(x :  2000 size-is x)
```

and PROLOG should deliver the required result.

```
1985 size-is 500
x size-is y if
              x after 1985  &
              z year-previous-to x  &
              z size-is y1  &
              y fifteen-percent-more-than y1

x after 1985 if 1985 LESS x

x year-previous-to y if SUM(x 1 y)

x fifteen-percent-more-than y if
              TIMES(0.15 y z) &
              SUM(y z x)
```

Fig. 7.7 The completed program.

Looking back at the solution

(1) Is the result correct? A query such as

```
which(x : 1987 size-is x)
```

(or with some other year for which the answer is known) should help to raise our confidence in PROLOG's answer. A full check will require you to do a lot of arithmetic (or a little mathematics).

(2) This problem provided a simple example of **modelling**. A model is a simplified description of a real event or process; our model was concerned with the changing size of a colony of rabbits over a period of time. Although models simplify reality, they should be accurate in essential aspects so that useful predictions can be made with them. By modelling with a computer it should become easy to answer 'What if... ' type questions. For example: 'If, instead of 15% growth, the rabbit colony declines by 10% each year, and if a colony of under 50 rabbits is regarded as extinct, in what year will the colony in Briar's Wood become extinct?'. Unfortunately, the program we have written is not powerful enough to cope with a question like this: the assumption of 15% growth is too closely built into it. A better approach would either make the growth rate a third, variable, argument of the `size-is` relation, or alternatively would record the growth rate as a database fact.

Can you generalize the program in one of these ways?

(3) Notice how naturally the second, recursive, `size-is` rule arose from the English description of the colony's growth. It's instructive to experiment with this definition. Does it make any difference if the first `size-is` sentence is placed after the second? Or deleted entirely? What happens if the second and third conditions of the main `size-is` rule are interchanged? Can you explain PROLOG's behaviour in each case?

MAKING A GAZETTEER

Problem A geographer called George wants to use the computer to store and retrieve facts about the world. Ease of use is to be a major consideration. He wants to be able to type the name of a country and get back the names of the corresponding capital city, the continent and the major organizations to which the country belongs. To show you the kind of thing he has in mind, the geographer has drawn a sketch (Figure 7.8) of how he would like the screen to appear in use.

Can you write a program to provide this 'gazetteer'?

Fig. 7.8

Understanding the problem

We have a **problem-to-do**. What is required is that the computer should carry out the procedure which has been specified by the geographer. This procedure can be described by a sequence of four steps, as follows:

(1) Ask which country the user is interested in.
(2) Get hold of the information for that country.
(3) Reveal this information on the screen.
(4) Repeat the above procedure.

When will it end? According to what we have written here, the procedure will carry on forever. If the geographer wants to do something different with his computer, he can switch off and start afresh!

Devising a plan

Clearly, our program will require some information about various countries; specifically, for each country we need the names of the continent, the capital city and the organizations to which the country belongs. On page 72, we saw that structured information such as this can be represented with a list; we shall follow that advice here. The information required about (say) the UK could be written as

```
(UK  Europe  London  (EEC NATO Commonwealth))
```

and in general, the structure

```
(COUNTRY  CONTINENT  CAPITAL  (ORGANIZATIONS))
```

looks like a reasonable choice. Each such list might be called a country's `record`, and following this idea we can store the information in database facts like these:

```
(UK  Europe  London  (EEC NATO Commonwealth)) is-record
(France  Europe  Paris  (EEC)) is-record
(GDR  Europe  Berlin  (Comecon Warsaw-Pact)) is-record
(Italy Europe Rome (NATO EEC)) is-record
```

and so on. As many facts like these as are necessary can be typed into the database using the `add` command (the geographer might even do this for himself). Notice, by the way, that these facts can be represented either by `X is-record` or by `(_x1_x2_x3_x4_) is-record`, and we shall feel free to use whichever seems most convenient.

What is the goal? We must choose a name for the procedure which is to be carried out. Almost any name will do, as long as it is sensible and has an atomic form. Let us choose, say:

```
gazette open
```

(where `open` is a postfix predicate with `gazette` as its single argument). The procedure has the four steps which we listed above. So translating into PROLOG, we can write

```
gazette open if
              x is-country-asked  &
              y is-known-about x  &
              y is-revealed  &
              gazette open
```

This sentence is 'non-logical' — it has to be understood in procedural terms. Notice that we require PROLOG to evaluate the conditions in strict sequence, and so we must ensure that they always succeed. Back-tracking is to be avoided here at all costs!

The last condition of the above rule will cause the same rule to be applied again. This is **endless recursion**; there will be no other sentence for `gazette open`, and so there is no way out. To get the program running, the query

```
is(gazette open)
```

should be entered. (Of course, this is not really a 'query' at all, but a command which activates the matching procedure.)

Figure 7.9 shows a flow diagram for the rule. The word 'gazette' is shown as an input to the `open` procedure, but it serves no useful purpose other than to satisfy a syntax requirement (a postfix atom must have one argument). An argument like this is sometimes called a 'dummy' argument.

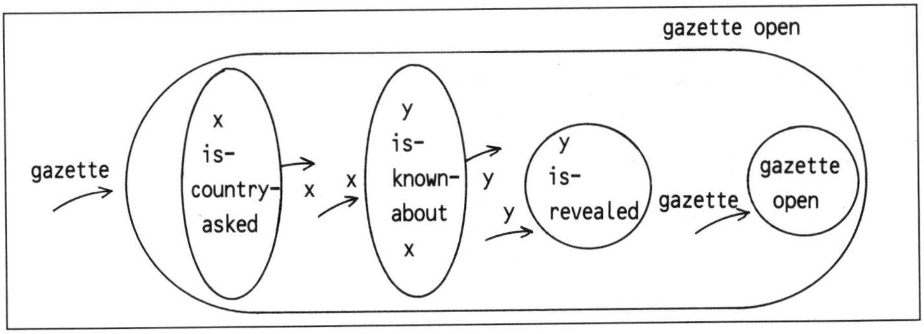

Fig. 7.9

We now have a definite plan. To make it work, we will need to define three relations: `is-country-asked` will supply the name of the country to be inquired into; `is-known-about` will supply the record for that country; and `is-revealed` will display that record on the screen.

Carrying out the plan

(1) `is-country-asked`

`x is-country-asked` is a procedure which we can describe with three steps:

(1) Print the question 'Which country?' on the screen.
(2) Read x as the user's reply.
(3) Move the cursor down three lines.

(The last step isn't essential, but it will make the screen a little tidier.) In the PROLOG version, we shall use the built-in relation P (Print) for the first condition, and R (Read) for the second. We met these relations on pages 67 and 68 respectively. The procedure can be written as

```
x is-country-asked if
                    P(Which country?)  &
                    R(x)  &
                    down(3)
```

where the down relation is one we will define shortly. Will it work? If you first enter the rule without the down condition, you can test it now. You should be able to try an interaction like this:

```
which(x :  x is-country-asked)
Which country? Spain
Spain
No (more) answers
```

(where the first Spain was typed by you at the keyboard).

(1.1) down

With this relation we have a small sub-plan to carry out. The procedure down(x), where x is a number, should have the effect of moving the screen cursor down x lines.

Can you think of a special case? The case when x equals one can be dealt with easily, since down(1) will be achieved if we carry out a single PP(). In PROLOG,

```
down(1) if PP()
```

In general, x will be greater than 1; down(x) will then require a single PP() to be followed by a moving down of x–1 lines. In PROLOG,

```
down(x) if
        1 LESS x  &
        PP()  &
        SUM(y 1 x)  &
        down(y)
```

Will it work? Enter the two sentences and try it — a query like

```
is(down(20))
```

will activate the `down` program and you should see the result.

(2) `is-known-about`

An example of this relationship is

```
(France  Europe  Paris  (EEC)) is-known-about France
```

and in general, `x is-known-about y` holds when `x` is the record for the country `y`. We can identify this record from the fact that `y` is its first parameter — for example, the `is-record` fact about the UK will start with the UK, the `is-record` fact for Spain will start with Spain, and so on. This suggests the PROLOG rule

```
(y z1 z2 z3) is-known-about y if (y z1 z2 z3) is-record
```

But what will happen if the user asks about a country for which no `is-record` fact exists — perhaps, a country which has not yet been added to the database, or a country which is misspelled? We don't want the `is-known-about` condition in the top level procedure ever to fail, and so we had better write a special case which matches this possibility. Let us add

```
() is-known-about y if not (y z1 z2 z3) is-record
```

to take care of it.

Will the above definition work as required by our plan? With a few `is-record` facts in the database, you can test it out with some queries such as

```
which(x :  x is-known-about UK)
which(x :  x is-known-about Transylvania)
```

and so on.

(3) `is-revealed`

The `is-revealed` procedure must display the information relating to the user's requested country on the screen. All but the first line of the screen shown in Figure 7.8 is to be generated by this procedure. The PROLOG definition is straightforward:

```
(x1 x2 x3 x4) is-revealed if
                              PP(x1 is in the continent of x2)  &
                              PP(x3 is the capital city)  &
                              PP(x1 belongs to x4)  &
                              screen hold
```

`screen hold` will invite the user to press key 'C' to continue, meanwhile holding the display fixed. Its definition gives us a small subplan which we shall carry out shortly.

However, we must not forget the special case. If the country requested was unidentifiable, then the argument of `is-revealed` is now the empty list. In that event the user should be kept informed:

```
() is-revealed if
                PP(No data is available for your country)  &
                screen hold
```

(3.1) `screen hold`

We can describe this procedure in four steps.
(1) Move the cursor down 5 lines (say).
(2) Print 'Press C to continue' on the screen.
(3) Read x as the user's reply.
(4) Clear the screen.

(Notice that we don't intend to check that key 'C', and not some other key, is the key which is pressed — any key with **RETURN** will have the same effect.)

The PROLOG version is

```
screen hold if
          down(5)  &
          P(Press C to continue)  &
          R(x)  &
          screen clear
```

`screen clear` is the procedure which actually clears the screen. Its definition will depend on whatever computer system you happen to be using, so you will need to consult your micro-PROLOG reference manual here. Once you have it, you should make up a suitable query to test first the `screen hold` and then the `is-revealed` definitions.

That completes the program. Just activate it with

```
is(gazette open)
```

and the geographer's problem should be solved!

Looking back at the solution

For convenience, the completed program is shown in Figure 7.10.

(1) Does the program meet with the geographer's specification? The only way to make sure is to test it thoroughly.

(2) In essence, all we have done is to 'package up' the information, making it available in an easy-to-use form. Instead of entering PROLOG queries, the geographer need only type the name of a country. The main price of this convenience is loss of power — there is no easy way, with our package, of listing all European countries which belong to the Warsaw Pact, for instance, whereas in PROLOG itself this would be no problem.

(3) Of course, although our program deals with geographical data, the method is general. There is no reason why it should not be modified to deal with information relating to a stamp collection, a club's membership list, or just about anything else.

(4) As with many **problems-to-do**, this one often forced us to think about PROLOG rules in a mainly procedural way. That is, the head of a rule is interpreted as giving the name and the arguments of a procedure, and the tail of the rule gives the sequence of steps which make up the procedure. A recursive rule like the one for `gazette open` produces a procedure which repeats. Back-tracking is usually unwanted, and we prevent it by making sure that the conditions of the rule always succeed.

```
gazette open if
        x is-country-asked  &
        y is-known-about x  &
        y is-revealed  &
        gazette open

x is-country-asked if
        P(Which country?)  &
        R(x)  &
        down(3)

down(1) if PP()
down(x) if
        1 LESS x  &
        PP()  &
        SUM(y 1 x)  &
        down(y)

() is-known-about y if not (y z1 z2 z3) is-record
(y z1 z2 z3) is-known-about y if (y z1 z2 z3) is-record

() is-revealed if
        PP(No data is available for your country)  &
        screen hold
(x1 x2 x3 x4) is-revealed if
        PP(x1 is in the continent of x2)  &
        PP(x3 is the capital city)  &
        PP(x1 belongs to x4)  &
        screen hold

screen hold if
        down(5)  &
        P(Press C to continue)  &
        R(x)  &
        screen clear

(UK Europe London (EEC NATO Commonwealth)) is-record
(France Europe Paris (EEC)) is-record
(GDR Europe Berlin (Comecon Warsaw-Pact)) is-record
(Italy Europe Rome (NATO EEC)) is-record
```

Fig. 7.10 The completed program.

(5) Activating the program by typing `is(gazette open)` is rather clumsy. Fortunately, there is a more elegant alternative. If you type `open gazette` you will find that this activates the program also. The explanation is that micro-PROLOG permits a postfix predicate to be used as a **command**: to issue the command, type the predicate first, and then the single argument. The effect is exactly like that of the corresponding `is`-query, except that PROLOG doesn't show `YES` or `NO` at the end of the evaluation of the goal. You can try out the idea with these commands, for instance:

```
clear screen
down 5
PP Hello
hold screen
```

(6) PROLOG programs as a rule consume computer memory whilst they are running, although the rate of consumption varies (and can be nil). The hope is always that our program will run to an end before the computer's memory does. However, the program we have just written has no end, and the evaluation of `gazette open` will eventually exhaust all available memory. On a small computer this may happen after the user has made fifty or so successive enquiries: at that point, PROLOG will abort with a `No space left` message. Then `open gazette` will have to be typed to get it going again. This problem can be fixed, but for us it isn't worth the bother. More important, and more interesting, problems lie ahead!

CONVERSATIONS WITH A COMPUTER

Problem Write a program which allows you to have a 'conversation' with the computer. Figure 7.11 shows the kind of exchange which should be possible. The lines with brackets were typed at the keyboard, and the others were generated by the machine.

```
(HELLO)
HI

(DO YOU WANT TO TALK)
NO I WANT TO SLEEP

(YOU MEAN YOU ARE TIRED)
I MEAN I AM TIRED

(YOU ARE A STUPID COMPUTER)
I AM A NICE COMPUTER
```

Fig. 7.11

Understanding the problem

This is a **problem-to-do**. What is required is that the computer should carry out the procedure which is suggested by the screen display. What steps make up this procedure? Evidently, there are three:

(1) Get whatever comment the human chooses to type.
(2) Give the computer's answer to this comment.
(3) Repeat this procedure.

Maybe you find it hard to imagine how the second of these steps could be achieved; but a close inspection of Figure 7.11 gives the game away. In each case, the computer's reply is just a modified version of whatever has been typed by the human. The two sentences in each exchange contain the same number of words, and moreover the computer's words are often identical to the corresponding human words. So the computer's answer is formed by echoing back the human comments, but with a few likely-looking substitutions: 'I' for 'YOU', 'SLEEP' for 'TALK', and so on. One or two details need to be worked out, but for now this insight is enough.

When will the conversation stop? As we have described the procedure, it never will stop. In theory the human and the computer will carry on talking until the world ends, although more realistically we expect that the human will go for some lunch before that happens.

Devising a plan

How can we represent the sentences entered by the human? As the sample conversation shows, we expect the human to enter each sentence as a list of words (including the brackets at each end). An unspecified such sentence can be represented by a variable such as `X`, say.

What is the goal? We must select a name for the procedure which is to be carried out. Almost any name will do, providing its form is atomic. Let us call it

```
talk more
```

(which is a legal atom, having `more` as a postfix predicate and `talk` as an argument). To obtain a definition of `talk more`, we need only translate into PROLOG the three steps which we set out above. A translation which seems reasonable is

```
talk more if
        X is-human-comment  &
        X answered-by-computer  &
        talk more
```

This rule should be understood as a procedure. The conditions are intended to be evaluated in strict sequence, and therefore we must ensure that they always succeed — back-tracking is definitely unwanted.

Notice that the third condition in the rule will ensure endless recursion (there being no other sentences which apply to `talk more`). This is something we usually try to avoid, but here it serves the useful purpose of keeping the conversation going (for ever!). To activate the program, we will enter

```
is(talk more)
```

Will it work? Certainly, it should. Our plan requires that we define two relations. `X is-human-comment` will succeed by replacing `X` with whatever sentence the human types in, and `X answered-by-computer` will succeed by making a suitable response to this sentence.

Carrying out the plan

(1) `is-human-comment`

`X is-human-comment` should hold if `X` is the sentence typed (in list form) at the keyboard. A single `R` condition (see page 68 for a reminder about the built-in Read relation) will be enough for the definition:

```
X is-human-comment if R(X)
```

Check that it works by entering a query such as

```
which(X :  X is-human-comment)
```

followed by any bracketed comment you choose to supply. The 'answer' to the query should be the **same** comment as the one you type!

(2) `answered-by-computer`

`X answered-by-computer` is a procedure which will respond in the manner described earlier to the human's list `X` of words. The easiest way to answer all the words in the list is to process the word at the head of the list, and then to answer all the words in the tail. This description suggests the rule

```
(y|Z) answered-by-computer if
                                  y is-processed  &
                                  Z answered-by-computer
```

Before we define `is-processed`, notice that the above description is recursive. Therefore, we need to supply a special, non-recursive case. The rule does not apply to the empty list of words: What happens if the human supplies that?

In fact, with the rule above **every** list will become empty eventually (when the whole sentence has been answered). So let us add

```
() answered-by-computer if PP()
```

The Print condition is not essential here; but Printing a blank line in answer to an empty list of words will make the appearance of the screen a little tidier.

Now we turn to the sub-plan of describing the `is-processed` procedure.

(2.1) `is-processed`

We will regard a word (taken from the human's comment) as being processed if it has been changed into some other word which is then printed on the screen. Of course, many words are not changed at all but stay the same; but for the sake of uniformity we shall regard these words as being 'changed' into themselves. The details of this can be worked out later.

Our English description of `is-processed` suggests the PROLOG definition

```
x is-processed if
                x changes-to y  &
                P(y)  &
                P(" ")
```

The third Print condition here will insert a space after each word. Notice that `P` and not `PP` is used — we don't want each word of the computer's answer to begin on a new line.

The definition of `changes-to` gives us a sub-sub-plan to carry out.

(2.1.1) `changes-to`

The choice of words which are to be changed is a matter for experiment. Here are the `changes-to` facts which produced the sample conversation shown earlier:

```
HELLO changes-to HI
DO changes-to NO
YOU changes-to I
TALK changes-to SLEEP
ARE changes-to AM
STUPID changes-to NICE
```

One other fact is necessary. To make sure that all other words are 'changed' into themselves, we should add

```
X changes-to X
```

Remember that when PROLOG is looking for sentences which match a goal, it searches the database from the top down. Hence, we should put this 'catch-all' fact last, since we only want it to be used if none of the others apply.

And that finishes the program. Make up some suitable queries first to try out our definition of `answered-by-computer`; try, for instance,

```
is((YOU ARE A STUPID COMPUTER) answered-by-computer)
```

and make sure you get `I AM A NICE COMPUTER` (or whatever) back in reply. If all is well, you can enter

```
is(talk more)
```

and then you can chatter away to your heart's content!

Looking back at the solution

The completed program is shown in Figure 7.12.

(1) How significant was the problem? It was good fun, but as far as a conversational partner is concerned we have to admit that the program is a dead loss. 'Talking' to it is like speaking to a parrot.

```
talk more if
            X is-human-comment  &
            X answered-by-computer  &
            talk more

 X is-human-comment if R(X)

() answered-by-computer if PP()
(y|Z) answered-by-computer if
            y is-processed  &
            Z answered-by-computer

x is-processed if
            x changes-to y  &
            P(y)  &
            P(" ")

HELLO changes-to HI
DO changes-to NO
YOU changes-to I
TALK changes-to SLEEP
ARE changes-to AM
STUPID changes-to NICE
X changes-to X
```

Fig. 7.12 The completed program.

The trouble is that our program has no knowledge of the correct structure of English sentences, and neither does it know what words and phrases actually **mean**. That is why the computer's answers will sometimes be ungrammatical, or senseless, or both. The problem of teaching computers to understand English is an important scientific problem, but it is an extremely complex one: our approach of word-for-word transformation is too simple-minded to get very far with it.

(2) Yet, without taking the program too seriously, we can make small improvements quite easily. We can double the rate of

word substitution by ensuring that SLEEP is replaced by TALK as well as TALK by SLEEP, for example. One way to do this is to replace the x changes-to y condition in the is-processed rule to x swops-to y (say), where swops-to is defined by

```
x swops-to y if x changes-to y
x swops-to y if y changes-to x
x swops-to x
```

and then delete the sentence X changes-to X. Can you see what this does?

Another improvement is to enable the computer to recognize that certain words belong to a category of words which can be treated alike. We can do this by adding some changes-to sentences which are rules. For example,

```
x changes-to GOOD if x is-bad
x changes-to PROLOG if x is-language
```

where the categories 'bad' and 'language' can be described by facts:

```
SILLY is-bad
CRAZY is-bad
MAD is-bad
...
ENGLISH is-language
FRENCH is-language
GERMAN is-language
...
```

and so on. Experiment with these modifications, and with any others which seem interesting.

(3) You probably noticed that we made two important assumptions: that the human will type each sentence in upper case, and that he/she will be willing to type the brackets. Sticking to upper case aided the identification of words, while the bracketed sentences made is-human-comment easy to define since the built-in Read relation can read a whole list at a time. Simplifications like these are very important. They mean that we can concentrate on the

important aspects of the problem without getting bogged down in detail. Now that the problem has been solved we could turn to these details if we wished, although it's doubtful if it's worth the bother.

(4) As described earlier (page 139(5)) the program can also be activated by entering the command **more talk**.

TIC-TAC-TOE

Problem Write a program which enables the computer to play a game of tic-tac-toe against a human player. The machine will play zeroes, and the human should be given the first move.

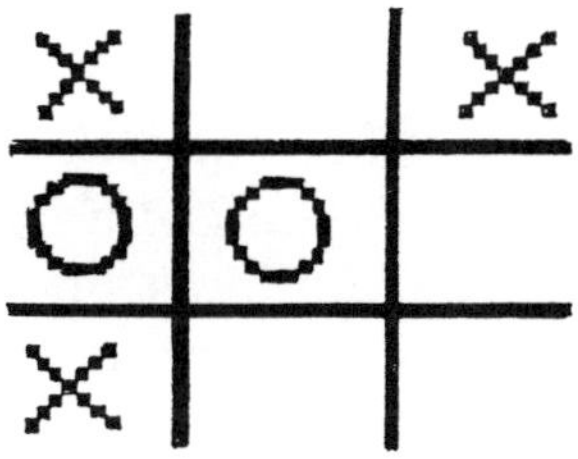

Fig. 7.13

Understanding the problem

A typical tic-tac-toe board in mid-play is shown in Figure 7.13. A good way to prepare yourself for this problem is to play a few games with a friend. Ask yourself with each move: **why** was that move a good move?

The problem is a **problem-to-do**. What is required is that the computer should carry out a procedure which corresponds to the actions of a tic-tac-toe player. Let us set down a sequence of steps which together make up this procedure:

(1) The human is given the current board and makes a move (if possible).

(2) The resulting board is now examined by the computer, which makes a move in reply (if possible).

(3) Repeat the above procedure with the new current board.

Notice that the board changes each time the procedure is carried out. In an ordinary game this corresponds to the piece of paper which is passed back and forth between the players; in computer terms, it suggests that the board is a variable parameter of the main procedure.

Devising a plan

How can the board be represented in PROLOG? Clearly, some kind of list structure is needed. For the board in Figure 7.13, let us write

```
((1 3 7) (4 5))
```

where Figure 7.14 shows how each square on the board is identified with a number. That is, we shall represent the board as a list of two lists, the first containing the numbers of the squares which are marked by Xs and the second containing the Os (the order inside these two lists does not matter). Think of this structure as

```
((HUMAN's Xs)  (COMPUTER's Os))
```

and notice that an unspecified board can now be represented either by a single variable `X`, say, or by a list structure like `(x y)`.

Obviously this representation of the board is only one of several alternatives, but it looks good for at least two reasons. First, it makes moves easy to describe: on the board `(X Y)` for example, a human X placed in some square `x` produces a new board which can be represented by `((x|X) Y)`. And second, we can easily test for a win — the board `(X Y)` is won for the computer, for instance, if the list `Y` contains a line of squares.

What is the goal of the problem? We must give a name to the head of the procedure which is to be carried out. Let us call it

```
X is-board-play
```

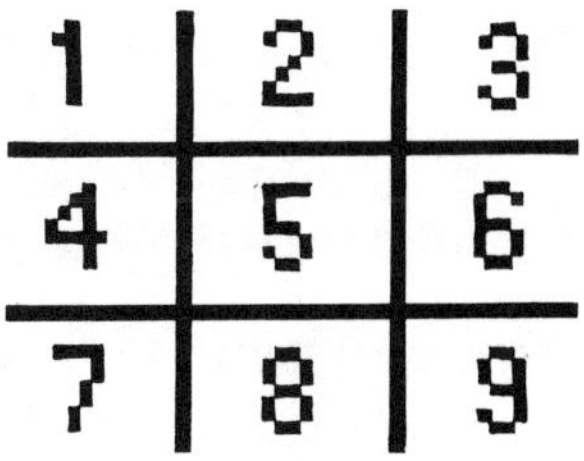

Fig. 7.14

where X represents the current board. We can describe this procedure by translating the three steps set out above into PROLOG. A reasonable translation is

```
X is-board-play if
                    X played-by-human-to Y  &
                    Y played-by-computer-to Z  &
                    Z is-board-play
```

Here, X represents the board offered to the human; Y is the board after the human's move, which is then faced by the computer; and Z is the board after the computer's reply — this is the board with which play continues. It appears from this rule that the game will carry on forever, but of course at some point it will become impossible for one or other side to play. Our intention is that the definitions of `played-by-human-to` and `played-by-computer-to` will both include a special case which will interrupt the game at this point.

Figure 7.15 is a flow diagram for the `is-board-play` rule. What will be the very first input X to the procedure? It will be the empty board, namely `(()())` in our representation, with which the game begins. In our plan, the program will be activated by the query

```
is( (()()) is-board-play)
```

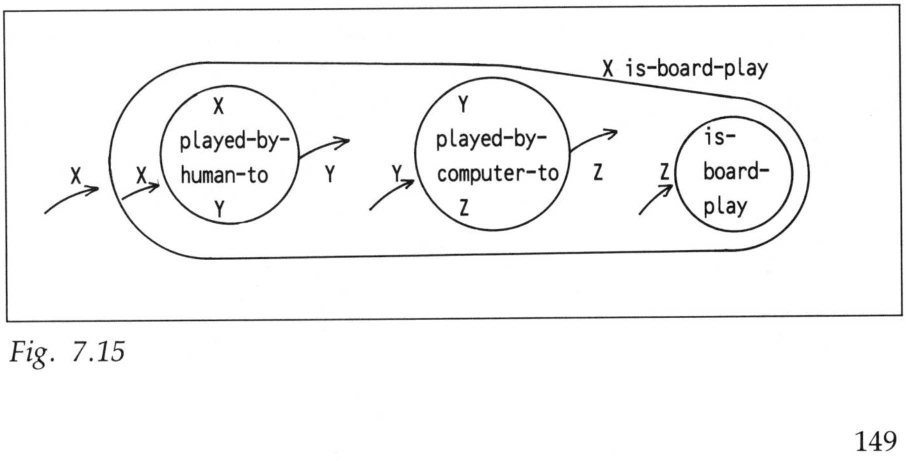

Fig. 7.15

Carrying out the plan

(1) played-by-human-to

Recall that (x1 y1) played-by-human-to (x2 y2) will hold if (x1 y1) and (x2 y2) respectively represent the board before and after the human's move. To define the relation we consider two cases.

(1) A special case: the board (x1 y1) may signify the end of the game. In that case the program should be aborted. What (x2 y2) becomes in that event doesn't matter: let us make it the empty list, say.

(2) Otherwise, print the question 'Your move is?' on the screen and read z (say) as the human's reply. In this case the board after the move is ((z|x1) y1).

In PROLOG, these cases can be translated into the two rules:

```
(x1 y1) played-by-human-to () if
                                    (x1 y1) is-game-end  &
                                    ABORT
(x1 y1) played-by-human-to ((z|x1) y1) if
                                    P(Your move is?)  &
                                    R(z)
```

ABORT is a special PROLOG built-in relation which interupts a running program. The is-game-end relation is one we turn to next.

(1.1) is-game-end

We should anticipate that this relation will also figure in the definition of played-by-computer-to. Let us identify three cases of (x y) is-game-end:

(1) If x contains a line of squares then the game ends and the human has won. A board such as ((1 2 3) (5 7)) comes into this category.

(2) Similarly, if y contains a line of squares then the game ends with a win for the computer.

(3) Otherwise, if the board `(x y)` is completely filled — that is, if no available square exists — then the game ends with a draw.

The PROLOG translation of each rule will include a Print condition to explain the outcome just before the **ABORT** takes place:

```
(x y) is-game-end if
                x contains-a-line  &
                PP(You win!)
(x y) is-game-end if
                y contains-a-line  &
                PP(I win!)
(x y) is-game-end if
                not z available-on (x y)  &
                PP(A draw!)
```

Here, the `contains-a-line` relation will check whether a given list of Os or Xs includes a winning trio; and `available-on` will attempt to find a square which has yet to be taken up on the current board. In these two, we have a sub-plan to carry out.

(1.1.1) `contains-a-line`

An example of this relation is `(1 7 3 2) contains-a-line`, since the list contains each member of the line 1–2–3. This example suggests the PROLOG definition:

```
X contains-a-line if
                (y1 y2 y3) is-a-line  &
                y1 member-of X  &
                y2 member-of X  &
                y3 member-of X
```

Here, `member-of` is the standard relation; but how can we define `is-a-line`? Fortunately, a tic-tac-toe board contains only eight different lines in all. It is feasible and simple to define the relation with a set of facts:

```
(1 2 3) is-a-line
(4 5 6) is-a-line
(7 8 9) is-a-line
(1 4 7) is-a-line
```

```
(2 5 8) is-a-line
(3 6 9) is-a-line
(1 5 9) is-a-line
(3 5 7) is-a-line
```

We can now test `contains-a-line` immediately. Try it out with a few queries such as

```
is((6 5 3 2 7) contains-a-line)
```

(1.1.2) `available-on`

x available-on (y z) should hold if `x` is a blank square on the board `(y z)`. An example is

```
6 available-on ((1 3 7) (4 5))
```

The obvious definition is

> x is available on the board (y z) if x is a square
> which is neither a member of y nor a member of z.

In PROLOG,

```
x available-on (y z) if
                        x is-a-square  &
                        not x member-of y  &
                        not x member-of z
```

It is important to our plan that `available-on` should be able to **generate** blank squares on a given board. Will this definition work? Figure 7.16 shows how it could. Notice that `is-a-square` must be able to output squares; the definition

```
x is-a-square if x member-of (1 2 3 4 5 6 7 8 9)
```

takes care of it at once.

At this point, some of our earlier definitions can be tested. Make up some suitable queries for `is-a-square`, `available-on`, `is-game-end` and `played-by-human-to` and check that they work as required by our plan.

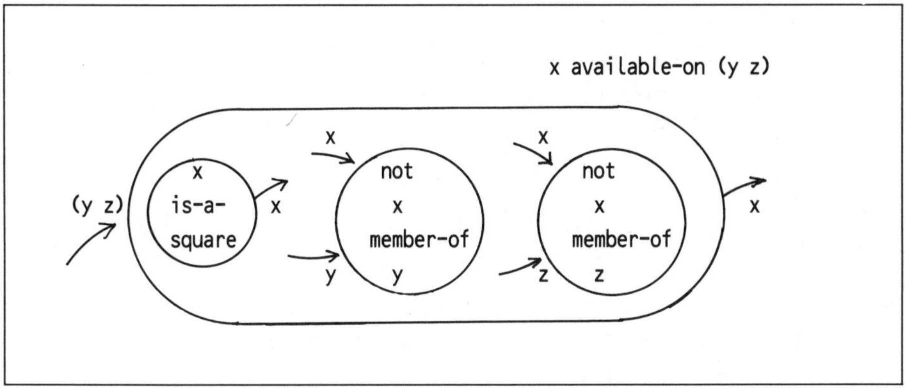

Fig. 7.16

(1.2) `played-by-computer-to`

`(x1 y1) played-by-computer-to (x2 y2)` should hold if `(x1 y1)` and `(x2 y2)` respectively represent the board before and after the computer's turn. As with `played-by-human-to`, there are two cases to describe:

(1) A special case: if the board `(x1 y1)` signifies the end of the game then the program should abort. In this case, denote the 'after' board by `()`, say.

(2) Otherwise, the 'after' board is `(x1 (z|y1))`, where `z` is some square identified by the computer as a good move to make on the board `(x1 y1)`.

Translating into PROLOG:

```
(x1 y1) played-by-computer-to () if
                                        (x1 y1) is-game-end &
                                        ABORT
(x1 y1) played-by-computer-to (x1 (z|y1)) if
                                        z good-move-on (x1 y1) &
                                        PP(I move to z)
```

Notice the Print condition in the main rule. It wouldn't do to have the computer keep its moves secret from its opponent!

Obviously, the `good-move-on` relation is crucial. Writing its definition involves a sub-plan which we turn to now.

(1.2.1) `good-move-on`

`x good-move-on (y z)` should hold if `x` is a suitable square on to which the computer could write a nought when `(y z)` represents the current board. Two examples are

```
6 good-move-on ((1 3 7) (4 5))
8 good-move-on ((5 2) (1))
```

(Can you see why these are sensible examples?) In our plan, it is essential that we write a definition of `good-move-on` which is capable of generating such moves.

Of course, it would not be practical to write a fact specifying a good move on every conceivable board. There are far too many possibilities. What we must do instead is describe a strategy for correct play on a general board represented by `(X Y)`, say; we shall first try to set down a strategy in English and then we shall convert it into PROLOG rules.

Here then is a general strategy, described in order of priority.

(1) If a square is available which would let the computer win immediately (because that square along with the computer's existing squares would contain a line) then take that square.

(2) If a square is available which would give the human a win on the next turn, block the human by taking that square.

(3) Take the center square, if it is available.

(4) Take any available corner square.

(5) Take any available square.

Are these rules sensible? Do they describe the expertise of an intelligent human player? At any rate, they will do for a start. Let us translate them into PROLOG, one by one:

```
z good-move-on (X Y) if
                        z available-on (X Y)  &
                        (z|Y) contains-a-line
z good-move-on (X Y) if
                        z available-on (X Y)  &
                        (z|X) contains-a-line
```

```
5 good-move-on (X Y) if 5 available-on (X Y)
z good-move-on (X Y) if
                  z available-on (X Y)  &
                  z is-a-corner
z good-move-on (X Y) if z available-on (X Y)
```

What about the priority of these rules? It's important that the first rule should be tried first, and only if that one fails should the second rule be considered; and so on. Fortunately, since PROLOG consults database sentences from the top downwards we need only ensure that the above rules are entered in the order shown to make the priority apply. (This is an occasion in which the order of sentences in the database **does** matter.) Notice that the last rule is a 'catch-all'; it will offer a move of some sort on a board with which no other rule applies. Refusing to move in tic-tac-toe is **not** allowed!

One new relation appears above, which we can deal with very quickly. For `is-a-corner`, we can write

```
x is-a-corner if x member-of (1 3 7 9)
```

Type in these definitions, and then make up at least one query designed to test each of the `good-move-on` rules. For example, the query

```
which(x :  x good-move-on ((1 3 7) (4 5)))
```

should put the first rule to the test.

The program is now complete. The only work left is to type in

```
is( (() ()) is-board-play)
```

and to see how well it performs!

Looking back at the solution

Figure 7.17 lists the completed program.

(1) By now you will have discovered that the program can be beaten. Can you write one further `good-move-on` rule which will make the computer play a perfect game?

```
X is-board-play if
                X played-by-human-to Y  &
                Y played-by-computer-to Z  &
                Z is-board-play

(x1 y1) played-by-human-to () if
                (x1 y1) is-game-end  &
                ABORT
(x1 y1) played-by-human-to ((z|x1) y1) if
                P(Your move is?)  &
                R(z)

(x y) is-game-end if
                x contains-a-line  &
                PP(You win!)
(x y) is-game-end if
                y contains-a-line  &
                PP(I win!)
(x y) is-game-end if
                not z available-on (x y)  &
                PP(A draw!)

x contains-a-line if
                (y1 y2 y3) is-a-line  &
                y1 member-of x  &
                y2 member-of x  &
                y3 member-of x

(1 2 3) is-a-line
(4 5 6) is-a-line
(7 8 9) is-a-line
(1 4 7) is-a-line
(2 5 8) is-a-line
```

Fig. 7.17 The completed program.

(2) Our program produces rather dull output. (It also allows cheating, but let's say no more about that!) It would be possible to replace the `PP(I move to z)` condition in the main `played-`

```
(3 6 9) is-a-line
(1 5 9) is-a-line
(3 5 7) is-a-line

x available-on (y z) if
                 x is-a-square  &
                 not x member-of y  &
                 not x member-of z

x is-a-square if x member-of (1 2 3 4 5 6 7 8 9)

(x1 y1) played-by-computer-to () if
                 (x1 y1) is-game-end  &
                 ABORT
(x1 y1) played-by-computer-to (x1 (z|y1)) if
                 z good-move-on (x1 y1)  &
                 PP(I move to z)


z good-move-on (X Y) if
                 z  available-on (X Y)  &
                 (z|Y) contains-a-line
z good-move-on (X Y) if
                 z available-on (X Y)  &
                 (z|X) contains-a-line
5 good-move-on (X Y) if 5 available-on (X Y)
z good-move-on (X Y) if
                 z available-on (X Y)  &
                 z is-a-corner
z good-move-on (X Y) if z available-on (X Y)

x is-a-corner if x member-of (1 3 7 9)
```

Fig. 7.17 The completed program (continued).

`by-computer-to` rule with a condition `(x1 (z|y1)) is-shown`, say, where `is-shown` would display a picture of the board; but this is only 'cosmetic'. A pretty screen is not necessary for solving the problem.

(3) The expertise contained within the `good-move-on` rules enabled the computer to play with some intelligence. A different approach is one in which the computer explores the effect of every available move, ideally looking as far ahead as the end of the game, and selects the best move it can find. This alternative is called **brute-search**. The question of whether to use expertise or brute-search often arises in game-playing programs: each has its plus and minus points. Expertise can be difficult to get hold of (imagine trying to write `good-move-on` rules for the game of chess, for example), whereas brute-search is often too demanding of computing power — even with a simple game like tic-tac-toe, a small computer may be overwhelmed by the number of combinations which a brute-search strategy requires to explore.

CROSSING A RIVER

Problem A farmer is on the south bank of a river along with a wolf, a goat and a cabbage, all of which he wishes to transfer to the north bank (see Figure 7.18). There is a small boat with which he can cross either by himself, or with at most one of his possessions. Unfortunately, if he leaves the wolf alone with the goat then the wolf will eat the goat; and if he leaves the goat alone with the cabbage, then the goat will eat the cabbage.

How can the crossing be safely completed?

Understanding the problem

Let us experiment with a few steps of an attempted solution.

Starting state	Everyone is on the south bank. Peace reigns.
First action	Suppose the farmer rows across with the goat.
New state	Goat and farmer are on the north bank, wolf and cabbage are on the south. Peaceful.
Next action	Suppose the farmer crosses by himself.
New state	Goat is on the north bank, farmer, wolf and cabbage are on the south. Peaceful.

Fig. 7.18

Next action Suppose the farmer crosses with the wolf.
New state Farmer, wolf and goat are on the north bank, cabbage is on the south. Peaceful.
Next action Suppose the farmer crosses by himself.
New state Wolf and goat are on the north bank, farmer and cabbage are on the south. Not peaceful — wolf eats goat.

Our attempt didn't succeed, but that doesn't matter. The point of an exercise like this is that it helps us to understand the problem. Clearly, the notions of a **state** and an **action** are crucial here: the states describe where everything is, and the actions describe what happens next. Each action transforms the existing state into a different state, which may or may not be a peaceful state. Let us call an action which transforms one peaceful state into another a **legal** action.

This is a **problem-to-find**. What is required? It is a particular sequence of actions. What is the condition? The actions must all be legal actions which end in the state in which everyone is on the north bank.

Devising a plan

How can we represent the objects in the river-crossing problem? The words `farmer`, `wolf`, `goat` and `cabbage` will denote the participants. What about the actions and the states? There are only four actions; let us represent them as

```
(farmer rows himself)
(farmer rows wolf)
(farmer rows goat)
(farmer rows cabbage)
```

The states describe the positions of the participants. Letting N and S denote the north and south banks, it seems reasonable to write, say,

```
(S N N S)
```

to indicate the state in which the farmer, wolf, goat and cabbage are on the south, north, north and south banks respectively.

What is the goal? What we are looking for is some special sequence of actions. Let us represent this unknown sequence by a list X, say. Then we can write the goal as

```
X is-solution
```

which must be solved for X (see Figure 7.19). The required list X will look something like

```
((farmer rows goat) (farmer rows wolf) (farmer rows himself))
```

only different! The condition for X which we identified above was that it must comprise legal actions which result in all participants being placed on the north bank. This suggests the PROLOG rule

```
X is-solution if X are-legal-actions-resulting-in (N N N N)
```

Can we write a definition for are-legal-actions-resulting-in which can generate the actions which lead to a given state? If so, then we should be able to query

```
which(X :  X is-solution)
```

and get back the answer to the river-crossing problem. Otherwise, we will have to think of a different plan.

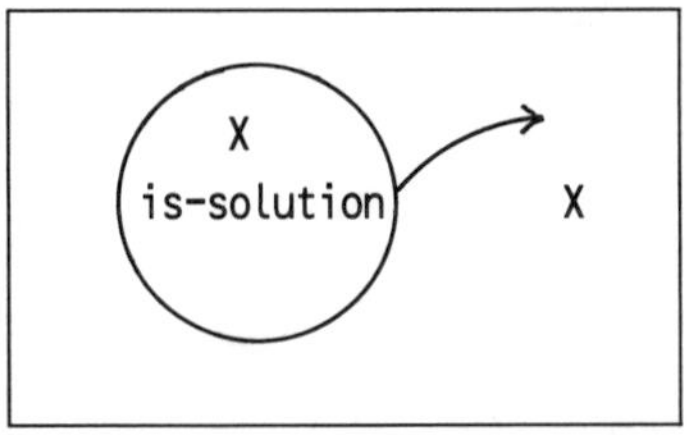

Fig. 7.19

Carrying out the plan

(1) `are-legal-actions-resulting-in`

It isn't too hard to think up an example of this relation. For instance

```
((farmer rows wolf) (farmer rows himself) (farmer rows goat))
                          are-legal-actions-resulting-in (N N N S)
```

these being the first three actions in the sequence we experimented with earlier, but with the earlier actions shown on the **right** of the list (this is the order we'll find to be most convenient). Does the relation have an obvious special case? Yes: there is the case where the list of actions is empty. This corresponds to the very start of the problem, when the farmer has yet to do anything and everyone is still on the south bank. In PROLOG

```
() are-legal-actions-resulting-in (S S S S)
```

Now it seems natural to look for a description of the state `z`, say, which is the outcome of a general (i.e. non-empty) list of actions such as `(x|Y)`. Is there a recursive description of this general case? How is `z` related to `x` (the most recent action) and to the state which is brought about by the list of actions `Y`? A good description of the relation is

> `(x|Y)` are legal actions resulting in the state `z` if `Y` are legal actions resulting in some state `z1`, say, and if the action `x` transforms the state `z1` into `z`, where `z` is peaceful.

Notice the last condition. Unless `z` is peaceful, then the actions `(x|Y)` will not be legal even though all the actions of `Y` were legal actions.

Translating into PROLOG gives

```
(x|Y) are-legal-actions-resulting-in z if
                                      Y are-legal-actions-resulting-in z1  &
                                      x transforms (z1 to z)  &
                                      z is-peaceful
```

Logically, this looks correct. But will it work? An encouraging sign is that we have defined the state produced by longer lists of actions in terms of the state produced by shorter ones. The special case gives the state corresponding to the empty list of actions, so PROLOG should be able to build on that.

Our plan has produced a sub-plan. We must define with the `transforms` relation the effect of each action upon a given state, and `is-peaceful` should check that a given state is a peaceful state.

(1.1) `transforms`

An example of the relationship is

```
(farmer rows himself) transforms ((N N N N) to (S N N N))
```

There are four different actions, so let us write a rule to describe how each one transforms the existing state.

(1) When the farmer rows himself, the only change in state is that the farmer moves to the opposite bank.

(2) When the farmer rows the wolf, the change in state is that the farmer and the wolf move to the opposite bank. (But this rule only applies if the farmer is on the same bank as the wolf to begin with.)

(3) When the farmer rows the goat, a similar rule to (2) applies but with 'goat' replacing 'wolf'.

(4) When the farmer rows the cabbage, a similar rule to (2) applies but with 'cabbage' replacing 'wolf'.

Translating into PROLOG, these rules become

```
(farmer rows himself) transforms ((X z1 z2 z3) to (Y z1 z2 z3))
                                                   if X opposite Y
```

```
(farmer rows wolf) transforms ((X X z1 z2) to (Y Y z1 z2))
                                                   if X opposite Y

(farmer rows goat) transforms ((X z1 X z2) to (Y z1 Y z2))
                                                   if X opposite Y

(farmer rows cabbage) transforms ((X z1 z2 X) to (Y z1 z2 Y))
                                                   if X opposite Y
```

Notice how the patterns `(X X z1 z2)` and `(Y Y z1 z2)` in the second rule (for instance) ensure that the rule will apply only if the farmer and the wolf are on the same bank. (Notice also that the word 'to' in all these rules is a dummy parameter — it serves no purpose except to make the rules easier to read.)

The `opposite` relation can be disposed of with two facts:

```
N opposite S
S opposite N
```

We can test this definition immediately. Try it out with a few queries such as

```
which(x :  (farmer rows goat) transforms ((N S N N) to x))
```

(1.2) `is-peaceful`

`X is-peaceful` holds if `X` is a peaceful state. Since the farmer and the wolf are never at risk, a peaceful state is one which is safe for both the goat and the cabbage. In PROLOG, we can write

```
X is-peaceful if
                X safe-for-goat  &
                X safe-for-cabbage
```

Now of course we must define the meaning of `safe-for-goat` and `safe-for-cabbage`.

(1.2.1) `safe-for-goat`

Two examples are `(N N N S) safe-for-goat` and `(N N S N) safe-for-goat`. Why is the goat safe in these states? In the first case it is because the goat is on the same bank as the farmer. Such a state can be identified by the pattern `(X z1 X z2)`. In the second case, the wolf is on the opposite bank from the goat, and here the position of the farmer is immaterial. A state like this can be represented by `(z1 X Y z2)`, with the condition that `X` and `Y` are opposite banks. In PROLOG, these two cases become the rules

```
(X z1 X z2) safe-for-goat
(z1 X Y z2) safe-for-goat if X opposite Y
```

Test these definitions with some suitable queries.

(1.2.2) `safe-for-cabbage`

The rules here are similar to those for the goat: the cabbage is in a safe state if it is on the same side as the farmer, or if it is on the opposite side from the goat.

In PROLOG

```
(X z1 z2 X) safe-for-cabbage
(z1 z2 X Y) safe-for-cabbage if X opposite Y
```

Make sure that this definition, and the one for `is-peaceful`, works as it should.

And that completes the program. Enter

```
which(x :  x is-solution)
```

and the farmer's problem should be solved within a few moments. Don't forget that the answer list has to be read backwards!

Looking back at the solution

The finished program is shown in Figure 7.20.

(1) Is the result correct? Have you checked it?

(2) Why does the `which`-query repeatedly display the same answer? It is because there is more than one way with our description to find the answer, and on back-tracking PROLOG discovers the

```
X is-solution if X are-legal-actions-resulting-in (N N N N)

() are-legal-actions-resulting-in (S S S S)
(x|Y) are-legal-actions-resulting-in z if
                Y are-legal-actions-resulting-in z1  &
                x transforms (z1 to z)  &
                z is-peaceful

(farmer rows himself) transforms ((X z1 z2 z3) to (Y z1 z2 z3))
                if X opposite Y
(farmer rows wolf) transforms ((X X z1 z2) to (Y Y z1 z2))
                if X opposite Y
(farmer rows goat) transforms ((X z1 X z2) to (Y z1 Y z2))
                if X opposite Y
(farmer rows cabbage) transforms ((X z1 z2 X) to (Y z1 z2 Y))
                if X opposite Y

N opposite S
S opposite N

X is-peaceful if
                X safe-for-goat  &
                X safe-for-cabbage

(X z1 X z2) safe-for-goat
(z1 X Y z2) safe-for-goat if X opposite Y

(X z1 z2 X) safe-for-cabbage
(z1 z2 X Y) safe-for-cabbage if X opposite Y
```

Fig. 7.20 The completed program.

alternatives. The cause lies with our `safe-for-goat` and `safe-for-cabbage` rules; if you inspect the two `safe-for-goat` rules for example you will see that both rules can be used to prove that a state such as `(N S N S)` is a safe state for the goat. For the sake of efficiency, we should make the rules **exclusive** — that is, we should write them so that at most one of them succeeds with a given state. An easy way to do this is to add the condition `not z1 EQ Y` to the end of the second rule for each relation.

(3) It is useful to add a trace point such as `PP(Now looking at (x|Y))` on to the end of the `are-legal-actions-resulting-in` rule. If now you repeat the `which(x : x is-solution)` query, you will be able to watch the lists of actions generated by PROLOG as it tries to find the solution. You may be surprised to see how much time is wasted on hopeless efforts, such as rowing the goat across and then immediately rowing it back again! The trouble is that nothing in our description prevents this kind of stupidity — in fact there is so much scope for it that we should think ourselves fortunate that PROLOG ever finds an answer at all. In other problems we may not be so lucky, and the solution may be completely blocked by the weight of useless searching. The need then is to try to give PROLOG enough extra knowledge of the problem to guide it away from dead ends, so that only promising avenues are explored for solutions.

(4) It would be neater to be able to query

```
is(x is-solution & x is-shown)
```

(say), and have `is-shown` defined so as to display the actions vertically, one per line, starting with the first. Can you write a suitable definition for `is-shown`?

ROBOT NAVIGATION

Problem A robot is required to navigate around a warehouse. Because of the daily movement of goods, the floor plan of the warehouse changes frequently; a typical plan is shown in Figure 7.21, where the dots represent robot work stations and the lines indicate navigable passages between them. In the robot's internal database, Figure 7.21 would be represented by a set of facts such as

```
a joined-to b
b joined-to c
```

```
b joined-to d
d joined-to c
c joined-to e
```

The robot needs to be able to decide which routes connect pairs of points. For example, it should recognize that the sequence `e->c->d->b` represents one route from `e` to `b`.

Write a program which will prove, or disprove, that a given sequence is a route between two given points.

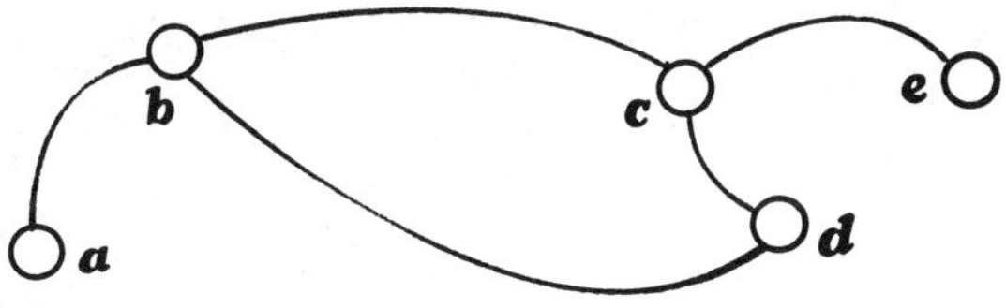

Fig. 7.21

Understanding the problem

Look again at what is asked. We will be **given** a sequence and **given** a pair of points. What is required is to `prove` (or disprove) that the sequence is a possible route between the two points. We don't have to **find** the route. So this is a **problem-to-prove**: the conjecture to be proved is that the given sequence is a route between the given points.

What exactly is meant by a route? Looking at Figure 7.21, it is useful to consider a few examples.

(1) Is the sequence `b->d->c` a route between `a` and `c`? Obviously not, since it starts at the wrong point.

(2) Is `d->c->e` a route between `d` and `b`? Of course not: it ends at the wrong point.

(3) Is `a->b->e` a route between `a` and `e`? No, because on the plan the points `b` and `e` are not directly linked.

For a given sequence of points to be a route between some particular pair of points, then, we can state three conditions.

(1) The sequence should begin with the first point of the pair.

(2) The sequence should end with the second point of the pair.

(3) The sequence should be connected — that is, consecutive points in the sequence should be linked points on the plan.

If these conditions all hold for a given sequence and a given pair of endpoints, then we can be sure that the sequence is a route between the points. That is to say, the conditions are **sufficient** to prove the conjecture. They are also **necessary** conditions, since if any one of them does not hold then the sequence cannot be a route: so we can **disprove** the conjecture also, by showing that the sequence does not satisfy all the conditions.

Devising a plan

How can we represent a sequence of points in PROLOG? The obvious answer is to use a list. The sequence `e->c->d->b` can become the list `(e c d b)`, and so on. A pair of endpoints can also be represented by a list, so that

```
(e c d b) is-route-between (e b)
```

will be an example of the relationship in which we are interested.

What is the goal? We can write it as `X is-route-between (y z)`, where a sequence `X` and a pair of endpoints `(y z)` will be supplied (see Figure 7.22). Our interest is in whether the goal then succeeds or fails.To write down a rule for `is-route-between`, we need only translate into PROLOG the three conditions which are set down above. A translation which looks reasonable is

```
X is-route-between (y z) if
                              X begins-with y  &
                              X ends-with z  &
                              X is-connected
```

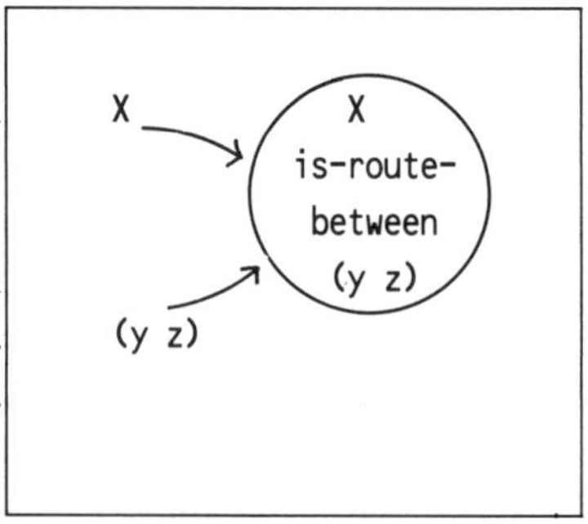

Fig. 7.22

Will it work? Figure 7.23 shows how it could. Provided we can write checking definitions for each of `begins-with`, `ends-with` and `is-connected`, we should be able to enter queries such as

```
is((a d e c b) is-route-between (a b))
```

and get a `YES` or `NO` answer back in return.

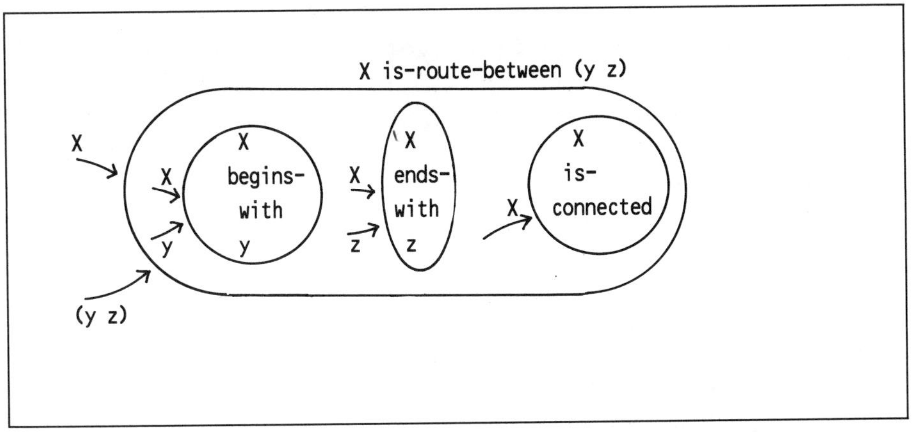

Fig. 7.23

Carrying out the plan

(1) `begins-with`

An example of the relationship is `(b a d) begins-with b`. Clearly for the relation to hold the endpoint must be identical to the head of the list. This description suggests the rule

```
(x|Y) begins-with x
```

Try it out with a few queries such as

```
is((b a d) begins-with b)
```

to make sure the definition works as required by our plan.

(2) `ends-with`

An example is `(b a d) ends-with d`. This relation isn't quite so easy to define as `begins-with`, because at first sight the last member of a list doesn't seem special like the first member. Yet, can you think of a list, one which is related to `(b a d)`, which begins with its last member? What about the 'reverse' list, `(d a b)`? Perhaps this suggests a description of `ends-with`:

The list X ends with y if the reverse of X begins with y.

On page 87 we met the standard `reverses-to` relation; we can use it here, along with the `begins-with` relation which we have just defined, to translate this description into PROLOG:

```
X ends-with y if
                X reverses-to Z  &
                Z begins-with y
```

Try it out with some suitable queries.

(3) `is-connected`

It isn't hard to write down a couple of examples of this relation. Using the diagram of Figure 7.21, for example, we can see that the list `(c d b a)` represents a connected sequence, whereas `(b d c e a)` does not. What about the general sequence, represented by `(x|Y)` say? What must be true about `x` for this to be a connected sequence? Clearly, `x` must be directly linked on the plan to whatever point appears next in the sequence; so let us bring this 'next' point into the open. Instead of `(x|Y)`, we shall represent the general sequence by `(x1 x2|Y)`, say; this is a connected sequence if `x1` is linked to `x2`, and if `(x2|Y)` is a connected sequence. (Note this second condition. Why would it not be sufficient to ask only that `Y` be connected?) So, let us write the rule

```
(x1 x2|Y) is-connected if
                x1 linked-to x2  &
                (x2|Y) is-connected
```

We have used `linked-to` instead of `joined-to` deliberately here. The `joined-to` facts given above assert that `a` is joined to `b`, for example, but there is no fact corresponding to the joining of `b` to `a`.

This is why `linked-to` is needed: it will enable PROLOG to make the obvious deduction. The two rules

```
x linked-to y if x joined-to y
x linked-to y if y joined-to x
```

will provide a suitable definition.

We cannot leave `is-connected` yet, however. The rule above is recursive, so we need a special, non-recursive case. Look at the rule again — what special case does it fail to provide for? The pattern `(x1 x2|Y)` represents a list of **two or more** members. A list of only one point is certainly 'connected', so let us add

```
(x) is-connected
```

This will provide a sentence which gives 'straight answers'.

Will it work? Try out these definitions with some suitable queries.

And that completes the program. All that remains is to check that our computer really can now solve the robot's navigation problems. Try out a few queries such as

```
is((d b c e) is-route-between (d e))
```

for example.

Looking back at the solution

The completed program is shown in Figure 7.24.

(1) How useful is the result? The problem we have tackled is more significant than you might think. The reason is that a diagram like the one in Figure 7.21 could represent much else apart from the layout of a warehouse. For example, it could depict a map of roads between towns; or part of a telecommunications network; or the bonding of atoms within a chemical compound. Mathematicians call any diagram like this, which shows a set of links between a set of points, a **graph**. For computers to solve problems in areas such as the ones mentioned, an ability to process graphs is a necessity.

(2) How powerful is our program? An obvious question to ask is

```
X is-route-between (y z) if
            X begins-with y  &
            X ends-with z    &
            X is-connected

(x|Y) begins-with x

X ends-with y if
            X reverses-to Z  &
            Z begins-with y

(x) is-connected
(x1 x2|Y) is-connected if
            x1 linked-to x2  &
            (x2|Y) is-connected

x linked-to y if x joined-to y
x linked-to y if y joined-to x
```

Fig. 7.24 The completed program.

whether it can solve the corresponding **problem-to-find**. That is, given a pair of endpoints will PROLOG be able to use our program to find all the routes between them? If so, then that would be a welcome bonus. Try out a query such as

```
which(X: X is-route-between (b d))
```

to find out. As you will discover, routes are generated — so many in fact that you will need to press **ESCAPE** to keep them from coming! — but almost all of them are routes such as `(b a b d)` which contain loops. In a sense this is only reasonable, since these routes do fit the description which we gave PROLOG; but probably we would prefer not to send the robot round in circles. We can banish routes which loop by adding the condition `not x1 member-of Y` to the end of the main `is-connected` rule. Now if you try the above query again, you will find that only non-looping routes are reported. Unfortunately PROLOG will not know when to give up looking for them, and you will still need to press **ESCAPE** eventually. So the free bonus is nearly, but not quite, attained.

SOME PROBLEMS SUGGESTED

One of the best ways to develop your problem-solving abilities is to practice solving problems.

The problems which follow are certainly not intended to steer you away from problems of your own choice or area of interest. They are simply offered as useful practice problems. The range of difficulty is roughly similar to that of the problems covered above.

Good luck!

(1) An insurance company maintains a database on which are stored thousands of facts of the form

```
(A R Robinson) born (12 7 1950)
```

However, errors crept in when the data was gathered and entered, with the result that some dates are incorrectly recorded. Many of these errors can be detected because they have produced dates which are invalid, such as `(3 15 1948)` which has too high a month, or `(12 12 1830)` which has too low a year, or `(29 2 1963)` which has too many days. Write a program which identifies individuals for whom the database contains an invalid birthdate.

(2) An historian called Linda wishes to use the computer to obtain details of events which occurred in any particular year. The system required must be easy to use, so that only the date has to be typed for the appropriate information to appear. To show you what she has in mind, the historian has made a sketch of the kind of screen she hopes to see (see Figure 7.25).

Write a program which meets her specification.

(3) A triangle may be described as scalene, isosceles, equilateral, acute, obtuse, or right-angled (at least two of these descriptions will apply). Write a program which, given the lengths of the three sides of a triangle, will supply an appropriate description.

```
What year? 1926

    Great Britain:
          General strike defeated
    Germany:
          Admitted to League of Nations
    China:
          Chiang Kai-shek takes over Koumintang


Press C to continue
```

Fig. 7.25

(4) Design and implement a computerized match-making system. The system will store a suitable description of various males and females known to you, and given the name of an individual it should apply appropriate rules to attempt to identify one or more likely partner.

(5) The sequence

1, 1, 2, 3, 5, 8, 13, 21, ...

in which the sum of two consecutive terms forms the next term, is known as a Fibonacci sequence. Given the first two terms of a Fibonacci sequence, write a program which finds other terms that belong to it.

(6) Twenty-four matches are grouped into three piles, initially containing 11, 7 and 6 matches respectively (see Figure 7.26). A **move** consists of a transferral of matches from one pile to another in such a way that the number of matches on the second pile doubles. Write a program which finds a way to create three equal piles of matches in three moves at most.

(7) Write programs for processing mathematical sets. For example, given two sets your programs should find the sets which are the

Fig. 7.26

union and the intersection of the two.

(8) A simple type of sentence in English has the grammatical structure noun phrase/verb phrase/noun phrase, as shown for example by: the early bird/catches/the worm. A noun phrase is an article followed by an adjective followed by a noun, or else an article followed by a noun; and a verb phrase is an adverb followed by a verb, or else a verb by itself.

Write a program which has access to a suitable vocabulary of articles, adjectives, nouns, adverbs and verbs, and which can generate arbitrary sentences having this structure.

(9) The eight queens puzzle is a classic chess puzzle. The aim is to set out eight queens on a chessboard in such a way that no queen threatens any other.

Write a program which finds solutions to the eight queens problem.

(10) Three black and three white coins are laid out on a grid contain-

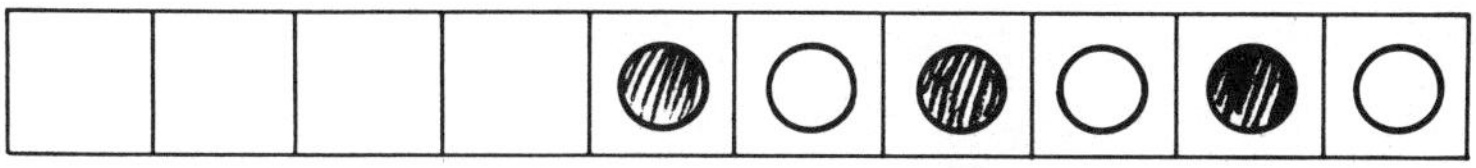

Fig. 7.27(a)

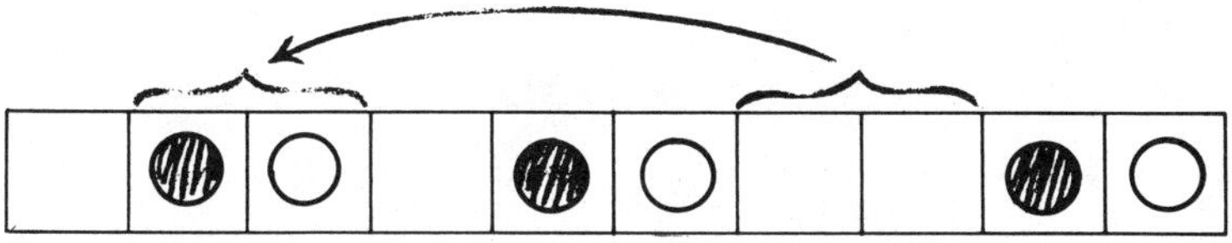

Fig. 7.27(b)

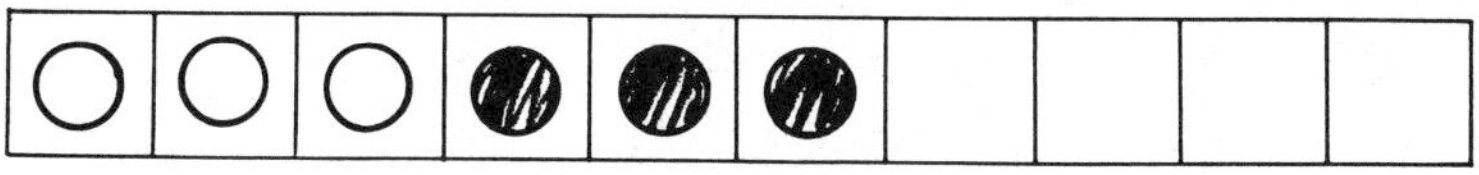

Fig. 7.27(c)

ing ten squares, as shown in Figure 7.27(a). A **move** consists of sliding any pair of adjacent coins to free squares (the coins may not be rotated or separated). For example, Figure 7.27(b) shows the arrangement of coins which would result from one possible choice of first move. The aim is to arrive at the state shown in Figure 7.27(c) within three moves.

Write a program to solve the puzzle.

Answers to exercises

Chapter 2

page 16

(a) is(likes(Diane Colin)) — YES
(b) is(enjoys(Jean rock)) — NO
(c) is(smokes(Ian)) — YES
(d) is(smokes(Janet)) — NO
(e) is(gives(Sam Colin cola)) — YES
(f) is(ill(Tom)) — NO
(g) is(ill(Janet)) — NO
(h) is(partners(Janet Ian)) — NO
(i) is(partners(Sam Diane)) — NO
(j) is(gives(Sam Jean white-wine)) — YES

page 20

(a) which(x : likes(x Ian)) — Janet.
(b) which(x : likes(Janet x)) — Ian.
(c) which(x : enjoys(Jean x)) — reggae.
(d) which(x : gives(Sam Colin x)) — cola.
(e) which(x : ill(x)) — no answers.
(f) which(x : partners(Jean x)) — Ian.
(g) which(x : enjoys(y x)) — rock, reggae, heavy-metal.
(h) which(x likes y : likes(x y)) —
Bill likes Jean, Diane likes Colin, Janet likes Ian.
(i) which(x : likes(y x) & smokes(x)) — Ian.
(j) which(x : smokes(x) & likes(x y)) — Diane.
(k) which(x partners y : partners(x y)) —
Jean partners Ian, Diane partners Sam.
(l) which(x : enjoys(x y) & not smokes(x)) — Jean.

page 24

(a) sensible(x) if likes(x Colin)
(b) glad(x) if likes(Janet x)
(c) hard-of-hearing(x) if enjoys(x heavy-metal)
(d) lively(x) if enjoys(x reggae)

(e) `expensive(x) if gives(Sam y x)`
(f) `jealous(Ian x) if likes(Diane x)`
(g) `odd(x) if smokes(x) & enjoys(x heavy-metal)`
(h) `detests(Sam x) if popular(x) & not smokes(x)`
(i) `remembers(x y) if partners(y x)`
(j) `miserable(x) if smokes(x) & not likes(z x)`

page 28

(a) `Jean partners Ian`
(b) `Janet ill if Janet smokes`
(c) `delivers(Santa presents)`
(d) `smiles(Mary) if rides(Mary bicycle)`
(e) `werewolf frightens x if x human & not x carries cross`
(f) `werewolf eats piglet`
(g) `is-sensible(y) if studies(y logic)`
(h) `retires(x) if age(x 65)`
(i) `grandchild-of(x y) if child-of(x z) & child-of(z y)`
(j) `lives-at(x Ten-Downing-Street) if is-prime-minister(x)`
(k) `y lives-on Wimbledon-Common if y is-a-womble`

Chapter 3

page 44

(a) succeeds
```
x= baseball.
which(x : x played-with bases)
```
(b) succeeds
```
y = Tony.
which(y : y plays soccer)
```
(c) succeeds
```
x = tennis; x = squash.
which(x : Alison plays x)
```
(d) succeeds
```
is(tennis played-with ball)
```
(e) fails
```
is(Tony plays tennis)
```
(f) fails
```
which(z :  hockey played-with z)
```
(g) succeeds
```
x = ball.
which(x : squash played-with x & baseball played-with x)
```

(h) succeeds

`x = squash, y = Helen; x = squash, y = Tony;`
`x = squash, y = Alison; x = tennis, y = Alison.`
`which(x y : x played-with racket & y plays x)`

(i) succeeds

`x = squash, y = racket; x = squash, y = ball.`
`which(x y : Helen plays x & x played-with y)`

(j) fails

`which(Y : Y plays tennis & Y plays baseball)`

(k) succeeds

`x1 = baseball, x2 = bat; x1 = baseball, x2 = ball;`
`x1 = baseball, x2 = bases.`
`which(x1 x2 : x1 played-with x2 & Ian plays x1)`

(l) succeeds

`is(not George plays squash)`

(m) succeeds

`x = soccer; x = baseball.`
`which(x : Tony plays x & not Alison plays x)`

page 49

(a) Applies. New goal: `George studies logic`
(b) Applies. New goal: `Rover is-a-dog`
(c) Applies. New goal statement: `Mary ill & x likes Mary`
(d) Does not apply.
(e) Applies with replacement `y = water`. New goal: `x type-of fish`
(f) Applies with replacement `x = bicycle`. New goal statement:
`Dibble friend-of Alison & Dibble owns bicycle`

Chapter 4

page 69

(a) succeeds with replacement `y = -1`
(b) fails
(c) succeeds
(d) succeeds with replacements `x = 6, y = 30`
(e) succeeds
(f) fails
(g) fails
(h) succeeds with replacements `z = 4, x = 1`
(i) succeeds with replacement `y = tomato`

Chapter 5

page 78

(a) `x = 1`
(b) `x = 1, y = 2, z = 3`
(c) fails
(d) fails
(e) `x = elf, Y = (eel auk dodo)`
(f) `x = pig, X = (cow)`
(g) `x = treacle, X = ()`
(h) fails
(i) `X = (dark handsome Tom)`
(j) `x = (1 1), Y = ((2 6) (-3 4))`
(k) `z = married, Z = ((Jones single) (Dibble married))`
(l) `x1 = fee, x2 = fi, X = (fo fum)`
(m) `x = oo, y = la, z = la, Z = (tum ti tum)`
(n) fails
(o) `x = treacle, y = treacle`

page 94

(a)
```
(x) product-is x
(x y|Z) product-is z1 if
                         (y|Z) product-is z2  &
                         TIMES(x z2 z1)
```

(b)
```
(x) is-uniform
(x x|Z) is-uniform if (x|Z) is-uniform
```

(c)
```
(x) is-ordered
(x y|Z) is-ordered if
                       x LESS y  &
                       (y|Z) is-ordered
```

(d)
```
(x) max-is x
(x y|Z) max-is z1 if
                      z2 bigger-of (x y)  &
                      (z2|Z) max-is z1

x bigger-of (x y) if y LESS x
y bigger-of (x y) if not y LESS x
```

(e)
```
(x y) adjacent-on (x y|Z)
(x y) adjacent-on (z|Z) if (x y) adjacent-on Z
```